THE BLESSINGS CAME INDIA-...

About the author

Grahame Dixon worked in the gas industry for thirty-eight years, until taking voluntary redundancy at the end of 1993 at the age of fifty-five.

He is a Methodist Local Preacher in the Batley Circuit of Leeds District. Since retiring, he has been awarded a Diploma in Clinical and Pastoral Counselling and become an accredited tutor with the Acorn Healing Trust, both of these skills being put to use.

He has been married to Marion for thirty-nine years, has three daughters and six grandchildren.

The Blessings Came India-Shaped

by

Grahame Dixon

The Pentland Press Limited
Edinburgh · Cambridge · Durham · USA

© Grahame Dixon 2000

First published in 1998 by
The Methodist Church
Dewsbury and Mirfield Circuit
Circuit Resource Centre and Office
74 Daisy Hill, Dewsbury
West Yorkshire WF13 1LS

This edition published in 2000 by
The Pentland Press Ltd.
1 Hutton Close
South Church
Bishop Auckland
Durham

British Library Cataloguing in Publication Data.
A catalogue record for this book is available
from the British Library.

ISBN 1 85821 736 9

Typeset by George Wishart & Associates, Whitley Bay.
Printed and bound by Antony Rowe Ltd., Chippenham.

This is the story of my visit to India in November and December, 1997. The visit was at the invitation of Rev. David Raju of Chirala in Andhra Pradesh State. He is in charge of a group by the name of 'Redemption', working in poor village communities to provide social and spiritual services to the people.

Our involvement was in preaching the gospel and sharing in the social work.

My story is in the form of a letter to my wife, Marion, and reflects my own feelings and stresses as I shared in this wonderful ministry.

All profits from the sale of the book will go to the work of Redemption, Chirala, India.

Grahame Dixon
May, 1998

*To my dear wife, Marion, who encouraged me to go to
India in spite of the pain it would cause her, because
she believed it to be God's will that I should go,*

and

In admiration of David Raju and his Redemption team,

With thanks to

*David's wife, Jemima, for her care of me during my stay
and the joy of meeting their family, together with Leonard
Nash and Robert Old for inviting me to share with them
in this ministry and for their support and friendship.*

Contents

List of Illustrations

Foreword

by Leonard Nash

It is a joy to write the *Foreword* to *The Blessings Came India-Shaped*, and to share a word about my friend, Grahame Dixon. This is a modern day story about God's call to common men to do an uncommon work in India. As you follow the author, may you get a *glimpse* of the *beauty and wonder of India.* May the Holy Spirit give you a *vision* of a *beautiful people hungering for God.*

This story revolves around A. David Raju, a native of India who has preached the Gospel for more than 22 years. After finishing school in India and graduate work in England, David married Jemima. Before the honeymoon was over, David would share with his young wife a vision that God had placed in his heart. The vision was *The Plight of the People with Leprosy.* David saw these as being rejected by government and forsaken by family. They wandered without organization, food, proper clothing, medication and shelter. '*I must go and help them*,' he told his wife. David did go to them and lived with these afflicted ones for 11 years. He organized them into one family. He sought help from all possible sources. A medical doctor from England came and witnessed the need, and through him a *Soup Kitchen* was built. Soon, medicine and other supplies flowed to the Leper Village from generous caring people of England. The present Administrator of the Leper Hospital told me that David Raju was the *Seed* of all that had been accomplished there.

After 11 years with the leprous people, God gave David another vision. This led to the birth of *REDEMPTION*, an organization that sought better living conditions: Clean drinking water, food, medicine and shelter for the people in the remote villages. The second level of his vision was to share the Gospel of Jesus Christ with his people. The third level of his vision was to Plant Churches and Sunday Schools where teaching and training would take place. After planting more than 20 Churches, David became discouraged because there were no strong leaders to keep them going. Where there is no shepherd the flock scatters.

For several years, David prayed that God would send someone to help him with this awesome task. In 1997, David received an invitation to attend the *World Conference on Hunger* in the United States – He found no help that would transfer to India. It was during this time that I met David Raju, and he invited me to come and help him with *Village Crusades*, hoping to fulfill his vision of establishing a School for Training Local Pastors, Evangelists, and Adult Sunday School Teachers.

Was God calling us in answer to David's tears and crying out for help? I felt fear and inadequacy for such an awesome task. God was not asking us to be mighty elephants, but *tiny ants*. Elephants can not separate the sugar from the sand. *Tiny ants can*. All that God was asking us to do was to tell the sweet story of Jesus Christ. My answer was, 'Yes Lord, but please send Grahame Dixon with me.' Of all the people that I knew, Grahame stood the tallest. 'He is a man filled with the Holy Spirit, a man of compassion to win souls for Jesus Christ. I rang him up and said, 'Grahame, the Lord wants you to go with me to India for *Village of Crusades*.' A few days later he replied, 'Yes, the Lord does want me to go to India.'

This book is a witness to the power and grace of our Lord in these latter days. Some may ask, 'Did these things really happen?' The answer is yes they did. Grahame and I experienced the *freshness* and the *power* of the *Holy Spirit* as hundreds came to know Jesus Christ as Lord and Saviour. Grahame has done a good job in describing the events. The work of the Holy Spirit is not so easy to describe. How do you document *Love, Joy, Happiness, Peace, Forgiveness, Salvation that sets one free from fear, death and hell?*

What is the Fruit of the Village Crusades? What Remains Today?

1. Land Purchased on the *Sea of Bengal* with nine buildings; Established School for 30 Handicapped Teenagers with four Staff members and Caretaker.
2. Campus Church building that will seat 2,500-3,000 people. The construction of New Kitchen, Dining Room, Bath Rooms and Dorms for students.
3. Construction of *Three New Village Churches*.
4. Bible Training Centre for teaching Local Pastors, Evangelists, and Adult Education. This School is under the leadership of an American Missionary, Brian Gammill and David Raju of India.

I am so grateful for Grahame Dixon's *The Blessings Came India-Shaped* for it is from a true heart. Pray that the witness of this book will open many doors that will lead to India. Always remember, God will use anyone that will help Him to separate the sugar from the sand.

Leonard D. Nash
Setting Sun Ministries
5420 Highway 128 South
Savannah, TN 38372 USA

Prologue

We had no idea at all what lay in store for us that day when Leonard Nash rang to ask me if I would accompany him on a mission to India. In fact, until then India was the last place on earth we had intended to visit.

It is difficult to say why I agreed to go except that I had an inner urge, which I can only explain as a prompting of the Holy Spirit, that I should go. Then you said that you thought it right that I should go and that confirmed it.

Now that I have returned, I am certain that it was right. I find it difficult to understand why God should choose me for this task. It has been such an honour to be of service to Him in this way, even though at no time could I describe the experience as 'enjoyable'. That there have been blessings is certain but the Scriptures which come to mind as I look back are Jesus in Gethsemane and 2 Corinthians, both of which are about blessings coming from suffering, although any suffering I endured is as nothing compared to these. Perhaps it is because I have been able to share a little in the sufferings of the people. I hope that the application of these Scriptures will become clear in my story.

Following my decision to go to India, I had a vision as clear as crystal. In that vision I was a wet piece of clay in God's hands and He formed me into a shape of India. It was a lesson that I would have to become India-shaped, that there would have to be no Western influence in my ministry there, but that I would have to live within the culture that I found and to come alongside people in their situation. This lesson has had a wider influence on my thinking on our mission at home, as I hope you will see later.

During my stay in India I have witnessed the madness of life in large cities such as Madras, the air thick with diesel fumes from inefficient engines in cars, three-wheeled taxis, buses, wagons and trucks and the roads crowded with not only all these vehicles, but with bicycles, rickshaws, ox-drawn carts, cows, pigs and dogs, all claiming their particular space of road and all contributing to the mayhem, heightened by the continuous sounding of horns. I have also seen little children, even those barely able to walk, begging on the streets and on trains, little children working in restaurants and elsewhere for a pittance, children sleeping rough without parents or a place to lay their head. I have been to a leper colony where I have seen those without fingers or toes, those with clubbed feet, and children who do not have leprosy but are destined never to move out of the colony. I have seen people using grass verges as the toilet, picked out in headlights as we have passed by. I have been to a country where hundreds of millions of people live without hope of anything better, due to a caste system which imprisons people in a standard of life which is no better than that of an animal, because if they rebel they are threatened with a religious belief that they could return as a rat. I have been in a country in which 98% of the population does not know the love of God in Jesus Christ and therefore has no hope, not only in this life but for all eternity.

The thrill in my visit comes from seeing a group of people who are doing something positive to deal with all these problems. It may seem that they are only scratching the surface, but the work they are doing is exceptional and worthy of all the support we can give them. It has been a privilege to see them in their work and to be a part of it for a while. I have seen children who would otherwise be on the streets being educated; whole communities being shown how to provide profitable work for each other and to work together in building industry and wealth; people working in the leper colony, bringing healing and purpose in life; projects bringing clean water and sanitation to villages and removing the need to reveal all to the world whenever they go to the toilet. I have seen the Gospel being proclaimed and witnessed the conversion of between 2,000 and 3,000 people, in one case the tearing out of a Hindu shrine because the whole village had turned to the one true God; churches being planted, people praising God with fervour and others crying out to God for salvation. People are living in new hope both for now and for eternity and seeing that their children have the possibility of enjoying a life far better than they have enjoyed.

I am now going to tell you all about it.

Blessing One

Off to India

The time had now arrived; it was time to go. Yesterday had been something special with that Service of Anointing for Leonard and me. Our Minister John had arranged the service and in it the whole congregation had prayed for us as John anointed us. He had also produced a prayer list for people to promise to pray for us at a particular time each day. The Church had sent us out; now it was time to say goodbye to you.

This was a new experience for us since we had never been separated for as long as this, and it was a sad moment for both of us. I left you in bed. I think that was wise as it meant there would be no long good-byes at the airport. Martin, our son-in-law, had arrived to take both Leonard and me to Manchester Airport. It was 7.10am when he arrived; I locked the door and dropped the key through the letter box. There was an air of finality about that. So that was it and off we went. At Margaret and Richard Ashworths' where Leonard had been staying, my brother Keith was waiting to say his good-byes. He was going into hospital on that day for an operation to deal with the Dupreyen's Contracture in his hand.

The traffic was very heavy on the M62 to Manchester and it was 9.30am before we arrived at Terminal 1 Domestic for our flight to Heathrow. We said our farewells to Martin and thanked him for looking after us as he did.

We had been able to book our luggage through to Madras, which was good as we would not have to handle it at Heathrow.

There were no window seats available but we were together by the aisle.

In the departure lounge I read a card you had given me:

'The Lord's unfailing love surrounds the man
who trusts in Him'. (Psalm 32 v 10)

'Safe in the arms of Jesus,
Safe on His gentle breast,
There, by His love o'ershaded,
Sweetly my soul shall rest.'

I filled up with emotion as I read it.

There was another card:

A Blessing on Leaving Home
As you leave your home
God in peace
go with you.
As you leave this shelter
God in power
protect you.
As you leave this love
God in love enfold you.
God bless and keep you
until in joy
we meet again.
David Adam

The plane set off a little late at 10.50am and we arrived at Heathrow Terminal 1 at about 11.15am. En route we enjoyed coffee and a sandwich. The transfer to Terminal 4 was by bus and we arrived at Departure Lounge 9 for the flight to Madras.

The BA 747-400 took off a little later than planned, but the Captain was quick to assure us that we would arrive in Madras on time. We had two seats next to the aisle again, this time with an Indian lady taking the window seat. I thought about your Self-help Depression Group, which was meeting at that time, and also of my brother Keith who was expecting to be having his operation then.

The Captain told us our route to Madras: Germany, Austria, Hungary, Rumania, Black Sea, Turkey, Lebanon, Saudi Arabia, Bombay, and so to Madras. The time in Madras was ahead of our own by five and a half hours. The Indian lady told us that the monsoon season was over and the Captain told us that the weather in Madras was good.

Before long we had a hot meal served. Lamb noisettes with a sweet by the name of Gulab jamon, a rather sweet and sticky cake in syrup. The menu was in English but also in an Indian language which the Indian lady told us was Hindi.

We settled down for the remainder of our flight. There were films being shown and various radio programmes available, but we simply rested.

Blessing Two

Arrival in Madras

The 747 touched down in Madras Chennai Airport at 4.15am local time. The tarmac was wet from recent rain which had now passed over. Passing through customs seemed to take an eternity but that was nothing compared to the time it took for our baggage to arrive. I met Judith Sykes waiting for the luggage. She was returning to Vellore, where she and her husband Tony are serving for the Baptist Missionary Society. They were at one time members of the same Church as ourselves and it was good to see her. She seemed sad, not surprisingly, as she had been home to see her father, who was suffering from cancer, and it was unlikely that she would see him again in this life. She did manage to ask me how you were and asked me to send her love. When we eventually received our luggage, somebody had taken mine off the carousel and left it there. Then Tony came to greet Judith. As we left the airport, Tony came to speak to me and we had a brief chat. I promised I would ring him later to see if it would be possible for us to meet again before we returned. This meeting with Tony was significant, as you will see later.

David Raju met us as we came out of customs. It was good to see him and meet him for the first time. He told us that he had arranged rooms for us at the YWCA in Madras and a taxi was waiting to take us there. We would be staying in Madras for two nights, since we had to wait for the arrival of Robert Old, an American pastor who had asked Leonard to join us here. He had been unable to arrange transport for the day we came.

The taxi ride was an eye-opener. Along the bumpy roads we went and arrived safely at the YWCA at about 7.30am. Eventually we were shown to our room, 213, a twin room with shower. It was plain but adequate and we slept until 10.00am, when for some reason the alarm sounded. We didn't realise at the time just how good this accommodation was.

This was the point at which we realised that our ride into Madras was as nothing compared with what was to come. We set off to try and find a bank for currency and a post office for aerograms. The sight outside the YWCA was unbelievable. What a noise! There was traffic of all descriptions, wagons, lorries, buses, taxi cabs, three-wheeled taxis, rickshaws, cattle-drawn carts and cars, all seemingly sounding horns and each trying to overtake the others by any means possible. It was completely chaotic!

We walked towards the oncoming traffic and eventually came to a Church where there were Scriptures painted on the boundary walls. This was Egmore Wesley Church. In we went and found the Pastor, Rev. B.J. Premiah. He told us that he had been there since 1991 and that one of his predecessors in 1919/20 had been Rev. Dr. Leslie Weatherhead. This famous author and churchman later became minister at Brunswick in Leeds, City Temple in London and President of the Methodist Conference as well as an eminent psychologist. The Pastor said that the Church was filled every Sunday. We gave thanks to God together.

Outside we met a man reading his Tamil Bible. He was reading Isaiah 51 and I immediately thought of the story of Philip and the Ethiopian eunuch in Acts 8. This man needed no explanations though. I discussed with him that chapter and those that follow it and said, 'Jesus is in it all!' 'Yes,' he said, 'Jesus is in all the Bible!' This man is Joshua Gabriel, a converted Muslim who came to faith in Christ seven years ago and is now an independent Pastor of a Church of thirty people made up of seven families. He is a lovely Christian man. He said that being a convert from Islam, he is a rarity.

We returned to the YWCA for lunch, having found no bank or post office. Lunch was western-style for us, soup followed by chicken leg, chips and vegetables. Leonard had to be careful with his food, having had a stroke some time ago, so we decided that from now on we would try the Indian-style food.

I managed to get a call to you after lunch. It was 7.00am at home and perhaps it was a bit early for you, but it was good to speak with you and let you know that I was OK. You seemed quite sad. Ruth, our minister's wife, had looked after you and it was good to know just how many there were back at home who wanted to help you. We said how much we loved each other.

We had a siesta until about 3.00pm and then we set off in a three-wheeled taxi to find the bank and post office. This was sheer mayhem! In and out of traffic, people and animals we went, within millimetres of other transport, motorbikes, cars, taxis, oxen and people. There were animals simply roaming the streets with nowhere else to go. I saw a three-wheeled taxi with the words 'Infant Jesus' on it and I waved to the driver; then another with the words 'Good Shepherd' and I waved again.

Eventually we arrived at the 'bank', which happened to be a Thomas Cook Exchange. Good! I had Thomas Cook cheques. £100 bought me a mountain of paper and off we went to find the post office. We found a dingy place, last painted almost certainly in the days of the British Raj. There I bought six aerograms at 5 rupees each (about 12p). Then off we went in another three-wheeler to the beach area.

This was something different; it was quite pleasant here. There were cows strolling on the promenade and others sunbathing on the grass. There were also goats and dogs about. 'Doesn't anybody own these animals?' I asked David. 'No', he said, 'they don't belong to anybody.' There was a group of young men playing cricket and we stopped to watch them for a while, and then further on we saw a statue of Ghandi which is quite impressive. On we walked until we came to the Basilica of St Thomas, in which is the tomb of the Apostle. Apparently Thomas came to India in about AD 50 and was martyred in about AD 75 and buried here.

We were standing in the footsteps of the one man Jesus invited to touch the wounds of the Cross. This was an awesome moment.

Another three-wheeler took us for another hair-raising adventure back to our base.

We noticed that a meeting was planned commencing at 6.00pm on the subject of the marginalised people, so we went along. We sat and waited but nobody came until 6.30pm. This is the style in India. It is known as 'India time'. Nobody ever arrives on time. The meeting began with a talk on Downs Syndrome, which was very interesting, but we could manage no more. We were worn out after a long day so we had dinner and off to our room to rest.

Leonard and I had a discussion on our reasons for being in India. He was concerned that perhaps we would not have as much opportunity to preach as he had hoped. He so much wanted to be in there doing what he had come to do and was wondering just how much we would be able to achieve. I said that we would have to be patient and wait on the Lord. David was there to be our guide and all would be revealed in good time. We read the Word together and prayed. We were in His hands, the best place of all. There was no way we could have anticipated what God had in store for us.

Blessing Three

Madras, Part Two

That night we slept well and David arrived at our room at 8.00am and led our prayers. We decided to go on a city tour. After breakfast David arranged the trip and said the coach would arrive in ten minutes. We were still naive about Indian time and we waited and waited. A full hour passed by but there was no coach. David suddenly decided to take us out and down the street. 'Might not the coach come while we are away?' I asked David. 'We have plenty of time,' he replied. What happened next was foolish and I was very angry with myself. David took us to a street-side coconut seller who chopped the top off a coconut with a knife of questionable cleanliness. That would have been OK since the knife had not been in contact with the inside of the coconut, but he then put a straw into the coconut and each of us in turn began sipping out the milk from our coconuts. 'How do I know this straw is sterile?' I asked somewhat gingerly. 'We don't,' said Leonard and we handed back our coconuts to the startled seller. David couldn't see the problem but it seemed that flies had been crawling all over the straws and we had no guarantee that they hadn't been used before.

We returned to YWCA and found that the coach had been and gone. I went back to our room sweating profusely and feeling unwell, so I took some stomach tablets. Leonard felt sickly and brought some of the coconut milk up and later so did I. I had taken Malaria tablets at breakfast and was unsure as to what I should do about it. I decided to leave it on the grounds that people who suffer

8

'Delhi belly' have no opportunity to take their tablets. There was no guidance on the packet of tablets. We prayed the Lord to protect us. I was so angry with myself.

We managed a light lunch and arranged a tour at 2.30pm. We wondered if the coach would come and wished that we were on our way to Chirala. Actually the coach arrived early but it was parked on the opposite side of the dual carriageway outside the YWCA. Getting across to it was an interesting exercise but we managed to do it.

The coach was in fact a rather old and rickety bus, although considerably better than some we had seen on the streets. We also had a seat. We have seen so many with passengers packed like sardines in a tin. Unfortunately the windows were filthy and when the sun was at our side of the bus, we could see nothing at all. It was very hot since the bus had no air conditioning, and we were wet through with perspiration.

Through the streets of mayhem we went until we arrived at our first stop, the National Museum. We wandered around the various exhibits. Leonard had taken some laxatives, which wasn't a very wise thing to do in Madras, and he needed a toilet. What a sight for sore eyes it was – absolutely filthy with excrement even in the urinals! Leonard decided to give it a miss.

Beggars are attracted to places like this. Even young children come smiling with their hands out. A young woman with a baby came to me. She was begging. She spoke very clearly in English and responded to everything I said to her. She was clearly educated. I said that I was unable to help her. It is difficult to handle these cases, but there are several reasons for not giving direct to beggars like this. One is that whatever is given to an individual, every other beggar demands the same and the situation becomes very nasty, as we were to learn later. Another is that this lady, so David told me, is a professional beggar and he feels strongly that people must learn to stand on their own feet. That is what he encourages people to do in

Chirala. It is far better helping those who are working among poor people, because they know best how to do it. I learned that lesson some years ago in Israel.

On we went to a modern temple-like building with gardens. It seems that it is used for large Hindu gatherings. There were more beggars, mostly young and fit people.

Next we went to the snake zoo. There was trouble here. We were stopped at the gate and told that we were not allowed to take photographs. 'That's OK,' we said, 'we won't take any photographs.' That was unsatisfactory from their point of view and they tried to take our equipment off us. We said that we weren't bothered about the snakes and rather than cause a problem we would wait outside. Eventually they produced a five-rupee ticket (8p) and we were allowed in. There was nothing worth photographing anyway.

We drove past St Thomas' Church. It was clear that our guide was a non-Christian, although over his head on the bus were the words 'Praise the Lord'. Instead we went on to a Hindu temple and shopping area. We decided to wait on the bus since we had seen enough for one tour.

We thought that by now we must be returning to the YWCA but there was more. It was dark by now and we were taken to the night-time beach market. There were hundreds of stalls all lit up by oil lamps and there was horse-riding on the beach. The guide gave us a full hour to have a look round the market but we told him we would make your own way back, which we did.

I had wanted to fast in order to clear my stomach and ensure it was OK but David thought I should take at least one malaria tablet, so at dinner I took both tablets. Leonard and I only managed soup. We weren't allowed to have bread. At the next table they were given bread with their soup and we asked why it was available for them and not for us. Apparently it was because they were having the full meal. We weren't able to have tea either, which seemed rather strange in India.

Robert Old was arriving at the airport at about midnight so we had to set off to meet him. We were surprised when the taxi driver turned right out of the YWCA directly into the oncoming traffic, which occupied the full width of the carriageway. One by one the other vehicles moved over and the taxi worked its way forward until there was a gap and he could switch to the other carriageway. I had never experienced that before.

Blessing Four

Robert Old Arrives

Robert's plane arrived just before midnight, according to schedule, and we were encouraged to see him in the passport queue within about fifteen minutes of touch-down. I had never met him before but Leonard had described him to me and it was easy to see which one he was, tall and bearded, very distinguished. That early encouragement was misplaced because his luggage was last to come off the carousel and our wait was a long one. It was good to meet our partner and off we set back to the YWCA, which we reached at about 2.00am.

This wasn't a very good night at all. I didn't sleep and my stomach felt distinctly groggy. I was also concerned about the malaria tablets, so much so that I rang the YWCA doctor next morning to seek his advice. He said that he would have to come and see me and would arrive at about 10.00am. He actually came at 10.20am, which by Indian standards is very good. I was pleased at my decision to ring him because he was very helpful even though he gave me a polite ticking off. He said that I shouldn't have taken the tablets. There is no malaria in Madras and he hadn't come across it there in thirty-five years of practice. He said I should wait until my stomach was better and prescribed some tablets to help it do so. All in all it cost me about £7.

Leonard and Robert set off with David to the Bible Institute in Madras whilst I recovered. They said it was a wonderful experience seeing students being taught to read the Scriptures and suggested that I ought to try to find time to go there on our return to Madras at the end of our visit. I never managed it.

We enjoyed a light lunch and booked out of the YWCA at about 3.00pm. We took a taxi to the railway station. What a mess that was! There were some porters in red skirts who picked up our cases and off they set. We were all out to keep up with them. At the train they asked far too much for the job they had done, more than would be reasonable back home, so David had to get into some bargaining. In the end he gave them something more reasonable and told them it was that or nothing.

Our first-class compartment was rather basic, but there were only the four of us in it. There were two benches with bunks above. The open windows had bars across to prevent theft and once we had closed and bolted the door we were secure, even if it made us feel like cattle in a truck. Little urchins, with hardly any clothing, came on the train begging, broad smiles across their faces. All this was hard to experience.

The train journey was quite comfortable, a smooth ride. The British did a good job in constructing the railways. We passed by some poor villages but this was mainly a rice-growing area, very green and wet. We used the bunks for part of the journey.

On the journey I asked David if he could teach me some Tilugu words which I could use when preaching. We tried interpreting some simple songs to see if the Tilugu interpretations would fit the tunes. We managed to put something together as you will see, and that time was well spent.

At 10.00pm, six hours after leaving Madras, we arrived in Chirala. Somebody got hold of my case. After the experience in Madras, nobody was going to do that, so I shouted, 'Hold on a minute', but David said, 'It's OK, he's a member of my team.' Then a real surprise. David's wife, Jemima, his son, Pradesh, daughter Santhi and many others greeted us and bedecked us with garlands. This was a lovely experience. I asked David to take our photographs.

They carried our cases across the tracks while we went over the footbridge, where we passed by many who were sleeping rough. David's jeep was there waiting for us to take us to his home. Jemima and the others followed in a rickshaw as we went through the narrow, pitted and sometimes unmade roads of Chirala. On our arrival at Baerpet, their home, David took us up the outside steps to the rooftop accommodation which was prepared for us.

Leonard and I were in the first room, which had two single beds pushed together, and Robert was in the second room, through which we went to the bathroom area. This had a western toilet, an eastern toilet, a shower room with a sink and a small area for changing. The longer we stayed in Chirala, the more we came to see how palatial our accommodation was. There were points for my electric shaver, which was nice.

Eventually supper was ready. There were all sorts of dishes but nothing seemed appetising. I had some rice and potatoes with jam and bread. It would take some time for me to face Indian food.

We had been made wonderfully welcome but there was a strong feeling that we were in a strange land. I wondered what on earth I was doing here.

We returned to our accommodation and I tried to ring home without success. I later found that the necessary connections weren't available at David's house. I wrote a letter and went to bed.

Blessing Five

Our First Day in Chirala

The first night had gone reasonably well and I had slept reasonably well. I had devotions with Robert this morning. I liked Robert from the start. He is an engineer and also pastors two churches, taking four services every Sunday. He is tall and kept banging his head on things.

David brought us tea and we asked for some bottled water with which to clean our teeth.

At breakfast we asked for toast but it came dipped in egg and fried. It was very much like the toast we saw Dustin Hoffman make in that tug-of-war film, *Kramer v Kramer.* I had plain bread and jam.

We gave out the presents we had brought with us and they were gladly received.

David's brother Robert, who lives in the adjoining house, came. He is a government-appointed social worker, providing services of health and education for children and their parents. He looks every inch an official. It seemed that we were going to see something of his work in Chirala.

Santhi, David and Jemima's youngest daughter, collected our washing and then helped Leonard thread some plastic illuminated crosses he had brought from America. He had brought about two thousand of these, so there was much threading to do. These crosses were very popular wherever we went.

Santhi is twelve years of age and is a lovely gentle girl with a beautiful face.

This morning it seemed that we had arrived. After daylight photographs had been taken of us with the garlands, we set off to see Robert's work. When we arrived, there was a class in session, many women with their little children but some fathers also. We were invited to sit down in front of the class and asked to speak, first Leonard, then me, and Robert Old last. I brought greetings from England, congratulations on fifty years of independence (which brought loud applause), thanks for the warmth of our reception, and pleasure in being amongst them. They sang what seemed to us to be a beautiful song about their land, our welcome and the desire that we would return. I sang the song in Tilugu, which I had learned on the train:

> *Wakati, Rindu, Moordu,*
> *Yesu nanu Praymisternadu,*
> *Wakati, rindu,*
> *Yesu ninu praymisternadu.*

which, being interpreted, means:

> *One, two, three,*
> *Jesus loves me,*
> *One, two,*
> *Jesus loves you.*

There was loud applause and smiles at my stumbling effort to use their language, but it encouraged me to sing the whole song in English with chorus in Tilugu.

We were then invited to present 'passports', documents indicating that parents had completed the course and granting certain future benefits to the children. After that I was asked to sing my song again. It seemed that learning that little song would be worthwhile.

Women then came to us asking for prayer both for themselves and their children, followed by the men also. My voice trembled as I recited the baptismal prayer from Numbers 6 v 24:

> *'The Lord bless you and keep you;*
> *The Lord make His face to shine upon you*
> *and be gracious unto you; The Lord lift up*
> *the light of His countenance upon you*
> *and give you peace.'*

We went back into the office and I asked for a translation of 'God bless you'.

> *Deyvudu ninu deevinchenugarka*
> *Yesu ninu deevinchenugarka*
> *Parishuddmarta ninu deevinchenugarka*
> *OK Deevudu ninu deevinchenugarka*

> *God bless you;*
> *Jesus bless you;*
> *The Holy Spirit bless you;*
> *The One God bless you.*

Robert told us about his work on behalf of the Indian Government, aimed at the poor and underprivileged, educating families and providing benefits such as health care, all supported by the World Bank.

When we came out of the office, there were more women queuing for prayer. One lady was suffering from nose bleeds. Leonard prayed in English and I pronounced the blessing in Tilugu.

This had been a wonderful morning. We gave out crosses to all who came, those with strings threaded we hung over their heads. I took mine off and put it over the head of a man. I felt that we had arrived.

Today we met Pradeep, David and Jemima's son. He is fifteen years of age, a quiet lad.

At about 5.00pm Santhi arrived at our door. She liked to spend time with us. I talked to her about her studies at school and showed her a book written by an American who had visited David and Jemima in 1984. Santhi read fluently the passages referring to Chirala.

Others came with tea and coffee and we all began threading more crosses.

Pradeep arrived with the letter he had received from Darren Lockwood, a member of our Sunday School, and which I had taken to India with me. He read it beautifully and said he would write back to Darren. Pradeep then showed me some of the algebra he is doing at school.

This afternoon people appeared at our door seeking prayer and crosses. We came out and prayed with them. They were parents of disabled children who had come to meet with David.

David came and asked us to join in the meeting on the roof outside our accommodation. David had received a grant from Germany to start a school immediately. At that time he had no accommodation for the children and was trying to secure some property for the school. He had budgeted about 600 rupees per month (about £10) for that, but it seemed that he might have to pay as much as 1,500 rupees per month (£25), the difference coming out of his own pocket.

The parents were wanting to ask questions about the school. David seemed to satisfy them. He has places allocated for thirty children.

Then a lady with a mentally handicapped little girl came and laid her at my feet. As she trembled and shook, I rose, not knowing what to say, so I prayed out in tongues and then over her mother and another lady. Leonard prayed over the girl also. This was a very moving experience. Lord, in my weakness grant me strength! It was so much like that incident which greeted Jesus as He came down the Mountain of Transfiguration.

David was unable to provide places for mentally ill children, but had promised that when God provided the resources, that little girl would have a place.

Shortly after that you rang. How lovely it was to hear your voice, but I was helpless to comfort you in your struggle. It was so painful being apart and we both wept profusely. You said that we would have a lovely December together and I thought how right you were. You were able to rejoice with me at the work God had done today. You were going to the Christian Endeavour tonight and Keith and Dianne had invited you for lunch on Sunday. On Saturday our daughter Jane was coming to see you, so you seemed to be well occupied. You asked if you could start raising money for David right away. 'Yes, please,' I said. Again we told each other how much we were in love. This was so emotional. You said you had received a grant of £500 for the banner group and I thought just how much further such a sum would go here.

You had heard from our friend Hazel and from the wife of a missionary recently returned to Nepal. Another friend rang you at bedtime every day. There was so much stress on you with many people demanding your time, but friends were doing their best to support you.

I reflected that I hoped you would have a good time in Scarborough next week where you had planned a few days with our friend Molly. I prayed for you over the phone and you for me.

More people came. This time it was the children themselves. One came walking on his knees. A fisherman had brought them, one of the fishermen who had been provided with nets by David Raju and who had brought to David the first fish he had caught as a thank-offering. David had tried to arrange operations for these

David Raju with Leonard Nash.

Garlanded on arrival in Chirala.

Garlanded with David, Santhi and Team.

Part of the Redemption Team.

disabled children, but so far in vain. He is now arranging the necessary funding and hopes to be in a position to do something about it.

It seems that David and Jemima were looking after these children in their own home until they could acquire the accommodation they needed. We noticed the children asleep outside David's front door.

We prayed for them and gave them crosses. We also blessed some ladies who came. It seemed that they were hungry for prayer.

We had dinner and returned to our rooms. This day which the Lord had made seemed like a week. I rejoiced in this man, David Raju. He deserves all the support we can give him. Thank You, Jesus for David.

This is his life's work.

Blessing Six

SATURDAY, 15TH NOVEMBER, 1997

Meeting the Team

This morning a meeting of David's team was planned and that meeting was to be in our room, so Leonard and I had to move our things out. Our devotional reading this morning was about Jesus being pressed in a room where He was staying. That came to life for us yesterday.

We were really respected here and I hoped that glory was going to the right place through our ministry.

David always stood by us when we were eating and as he did so this morning, I was really struggling – chapatis with jam on. Then I managed to peel and eat a red apple and drink black tea. David explained that in India guests always eat before the family. I was hoping that they could deal with all the food we were leaving.

After breakfast some group members arrived. One of them, Dhamaros, was going off to prepare for our visit on Monday. Leonard prayed for him and off he went.

David then welcomed us and introduced us to his team. There were twenty of them altogether, and each one in turn told us of their ministry.

Subaru is responsible for the recording of all the activity of the group. He provides photographs, video recordings, audio tapes etc. He is also involved in the fishing scheme in that he receives radar information concerning the location of fish stock so that he can direct fishermen to the appropriate areas.

Prasad, a Hindu, is the Office Manager, doing the accounting and typing work and producing reports. He has been with the group for seven years.

Suresh is a representative from Campus Crusade for Christ and is involved in showing the Jesus film based on the Gospel of St Luke. This film has been shown in more than seventy villages with some considerable success.

Franklin, who is deaf and dumb and yet has a BA degree, is learning office and computer work.

Anand, along with Serath and Solomon, is responsible for work in ten villages. They each work with the communities, identifying community problems and preparing programmes to achieve solutions. They are developing programmes for community savings schemes to purchase fishing nets, teaching people how to dry fish properly and to get a better price as a result. They help in providing water wells and sanitation with the help of Water Aid (a British charity), toilets and wash rooms, providing education for the children and health visitors for the whole community. They encourage people to contribute their own labour in lieu of money and they run skills development programmes such as repair of motors and business education so that the fisher folk can market their own fish without the need of a greedy middleman. They provide literacy programmes and teach how to read the Bible. Even Prasad, a Hindu, helps with this and through it is himself coming to faith. They are looking to help communities to become self-sufficient. In addition to all that, they help communities to build Churches. What happens is that those benefiting see Christians doing this work out of sheer love and for no gain for themselves. By this they are drawn to the God who motivates those who have come to help them. New Churches are constantly being opened.

Mamoharama (Fragrance), Anapurna, who is deaf, and Jeylekshmi (Victory of money) are nurses, each responsible for providing health care in ten villages. They visit ladies door to door as District Nurses, providing health education, personal hygiene, sanitation, disease prevention, etc. They say that children are the most vulnerable and they provide immunisation treatment.

These ladies also work with ladies' groups in villages with the savings schemes (kept separate from the men's schemes to ensure independence), in vegetable growing and purchasing fishing containers. Jeylekshmi also helps run a Sunday School.

Charlis is the driver. He is also involved, giving his testimony and playing the drums.

Krupa (Grace) is arranging the home for handicapped children and is the lady appointed to be in charge of it. Her husband, Salman, has volunteered but as yet is still being assessed concerning his suitability for the work.

David told us that he was trained at Bible School and had spent ten years with leprosy patients. He had found that too restrictive and felt a call to start his own organisation. He founded Redemption in 1988 and found the early months very difficult, especially with no income. He visited villages by bicycle, identifying problems and finding support where he could to do something about it.

Redemption gradually grew as an organisation, was given a jeep by the Swiss government, and his work continued to expand. He said that leprosy is still a problem in India.

Leonard spoke a word of encouragement, referring to David's visit to America, where they had met, and their discussion which had led to Leonard's desire to come and see David's work. Apparently David had not been so well received in America and had had to find accommodation in a hostel for drop-outs. Leonard had befriended him and invited him to his own Church. David had preached there with so much power and authority that people were coming forward in response in a way such as had never happened with his own preaching. Leonard had determined to come to India and support David in his work.

I then told them this was the Lord's work and marvellous to us. I promised that we would pray for them. Robert followed, speaking in admiration.

There followed a time of rejoicing in the Lord. They sang solos and together some of their Tilugu Christian songs and David explained them to us. Krupa sang, 'I have decided to follow Jesus' in English rather beautifully. I sang some choruses, 'Bless the Lord O my soul' with Leonard, then 'O give thanks' and 'A new commandment'. Two members had brought their drums so all our songs were sung to a beat and there was clapping also. What a blessing they would be to our music group at home!

Then, one by one, they told us of their vision. They were united in working for the good of the whole team, seeking to grow together spiritually and wanting to serve God in their lives. Some were still seeking faith and were honest enough to admit it. Salman said he had suffered from TB but was now healed and God had helped him. Krupa has had polio but God healed her and in consequence she has given her life to working among disabled children. Charlis was converted six years ago. He is involved with young people and enjoys the work. Prasad said that his office work wasn't the most important thing, but being part of the team.

David asked everyone to come back after lunch when the guests would each give encouragement from the Word of God. We thought it was very good of David to give us so much notice.

The three of us had a quick call-over and agreed that Robert would start, followed by me, and lastly, Leonard.

Robert spoke on John 1 referring to who Christ is and what He is about, and went on to speak of God's Word, the Scriptures.

I asked for the story of Jesus in Gethsemane to be read from the Tilugu Bible. I spoke of Jesus' humanity, of how He shared our human weaknesses and how in the garden He asked God to take away the Cross with all its pain. I told of how he responded in obedience, that He received the strength to go to that Cross and was able to cry out in triumph, 'It is finished!' God the Father agreed that it was finished and showed it by raising Jesus from the dead. In His obedience, Jesus had overcome the power of sin and death.

I went on to relate this to our earthly pilgrimage. God seeks people who are obedient to their calling and who, through their obedience, are empowered to live for Him. His will is expressed in the Commandments of Jesus, first to love God, to seek Him and trust Him and then to show that love in our love of others. I encouraged them in that they are showing their love of others in their wonderful work among the underprivileged.

Finally I reminded them that they were commanded to love themselves, to take care of their bodies, which are temples of the Holy Spirit, and to feed their minds with the things of God.

I told them that we would pray for them and their work and that at the end of their Redemption road and completion of their tasks, God would say, 'Well done, good and faithful servant'.

Leonard had read Luke 23 verses 33 and 34 and focused on the Cross, reminding his hearers that we find God there at the foot of that Cross. He talked about carrying our crosses and every day giving ourselves to Jesus.

He spoke of the Redemption ministry, of a team which needs to be focused and to agree together. It is not easy being a Christian but a wonderful calling.

We took some questions. Surprisingly the two we were asked concerned the last things and observance of the Sabbath.

People mixed around, some seeking prayer, others crosses. Salman came to tell us of his healing and that of his wife Krupa. He said he would like to have an English Bible. Leonard offered him a New Testament with Psalms but that was not what he wanted. He really wanted a Bible like my Thompson Chain-Reference Bible. I explained that a Bible like mine would cost in excess of 3,000 rupees (about £50) in England, and I could see the shock on his face. There is no way he could use a Bible like mine and 3,000 rupees would buy far more than a Bible in India. David said he would get a suitable Bible for him.

Santhi came to see us and asked if I would like to learn some Tilugu words. We tried writing down some sounds and then some simple words.

ama-	mummy
nana-	daddy
antamaru-	brother
anchelee	sister
tartaya	granddad
amama	grandma

I noticed that I had been bitten by a mosquito for the fifth time. This time the bite was on the edge of my ear. Santhi said that she is never bitten by mosquitoes. I already had two bites on my face, one on my hand and one at the back of my ankle.

dormalu cootinavee	mosquitoes bite
bargunara	how are you?
bargunanu	fine thank you

'Can I go now?' Santhi asked. 'Of course, thank you.'

Leonard was very persuasive in pressing David to accept payment for our keep but David would have none of it. He had invited us and would see to it that he would care for us and keep us. The only terms on which David would accept gifts was by accepting them for Redemption and not for himself or his family. Leonard gave him a substantial sum and began to talk about what was needed for the expansion of the work.

David's vision was for a school for handicapped children, a Bible school and an operations centre. They had eyes on a five-acre plot which they thought would cost about 250,000 rupees, about

£4,000. Leonard said he could raise that and encouraged David to go ahead. Of course much more would be needed for construction work or services and for operating costs, but this was truly an exciting vision. I wondered if there might be room for that little mentally ill child and others like her.

I wondered if all our days could possibly be like these last two. It was planned that tomorrow we would preach twice.

Blessing Seven

Our First Preaching Appointments

O ur reading this morning was 1 John Chapter 1. This was a lovely reading and had a good commentary to go with it. Robert was impressed with Selwyn Hughes' notes and looked for the American address. I promised he could take my copy home with him.

After breakfast we prepared for our services today and at 11.00am we set off in the Redemption jeep. I noticed that the Redemption logo on the door of the jeep was a map of India with a Bible and a fish on it and the words 'Redemption reaches the unreached'. This tied in exactly with the vision I had before I left home.

Through the narrow streets of Chirala we went, in daylight for the first time. The streets were busy with people, animals and traffic. The driver, Charlis, sounded the horn continuously as he tried to weave in and out of this medley. We had difficulty in passing a wagon coming towards us. Eventually we were on a country track between rice fields, with people, mainly women, carrying vegetables and other things. There was a dead dog covered with flies.

After about half an hour we arrived at a little Church. Songs were coming out over the loudspeakers. There was a man in the Church singing his heart out. Some people came to meet us and shake our hands. There were not many there. It seemed there had been a problem for the congregation and they had yet to arrive. Eventually David said that we would go on to another Church and come back to this one later. So on we went along bumpy tracks until a few minutes later we arrived at the second Church.

Here the congregation was in full swing and were ready for us. They sat us down behind the table and served us with Pepsi. This was usual practice. We were welcomed and I was asked to preach first.

I noticed that the men sat on one side of the Church with women and children on the other side. There were about one hundred people crowded in to the building.

I began by asking them how they were in Tilugu: *'bargunara?'* and the response came back: *'bargunanu'*.

Then I sang the song, *One, two, three, Jesus loves me*, the chorus in Tilugu and verses in English, getting the congregation to sing the chorus. Then I sang *Jesus loves the little children* and interpreted in speech since Tilugu words do not fit the tune. They seemed to appreciate that.

I preached on the Treasure and the Pearl, focusing on what God has done in Christ to purchase us and to make us into that pearl. I felt free with only an outline and I felt the power of God in my preaching in a way I have not noticed before, even though it was interspersed with David's interpretations.

Robert followed me. I was coming back to earth and not able to listen to what he had to say.

Leonard had not intended to speak but he came out bouncing and preached on prayer and the power that there is in prayer. He went on to ask if any wanted to commit their lives to Christ and eight people came.

As we left, I touched the heads of the children and prayed a blessing. Soon women came, heads covered, asking for prayer and it was some time before we were able to leave.

At 1.30pm we set off back to the other Church and when we arrived, the worship was in full swing, all guns blazing and coming out loud and clear over the loudspeakers. We left our footwear at the door and in we went.

Eventually two girls performed a lovely dance. It seems that they were expressing a welcome to us. There were seventy or eighty people in this place.

We were introduced and this time Robert was first to speak. He preached on 1 Corinthians 13, faith, hope and love and the greatest is love. God saves us because He loves us.

I followed. The first part was as before but this time I preached on Hebrews 3 v 3, 'Jesus has been found worthy of greater honour than Moses.' It took the form of a comparison of the works of deliverance and the two people concerned. At the end I mentioned Ghandi and fifty years of Indian independence. I said that Ghandi was not a Jesus. I was surprised there was no response at the mention of Ghandi's name but went on to invite them to follow Jesus and come to the Cross.

Leonard followed with the same message as before and the Pastor asked those who wanted to give their lives to Christ to put their hands up. There were twenty.

There followed much singing and then Communion. During Communion some women were weeping and calling out to God. The Pastor took round pieces of flat bread and brought some to us. Then he took wine, pouring it from a common cup into the open mouths. When he came to us, he took a separate cup. One of us refused the wine, the second drank it down without a thought and the third held it in his mouth until he decided whether it was safe, eventually drinking it down on the basis that it had been blessed. There were no after-effects.

We had been given bottles of Coke. One partly full bottle had attracted some flies and in trying to shoo them away, I knocked the bottle over. There were flies everywhere and it was made worse by a goat coming to the side door by which I was sitting and leaving some droppings. There were millions of flies all around and nobody else seemed to notice.

The singing went on and on. I think they were repeating the

same words over and over again, exciting themselves. I was unhappy with that. David had to tell them we needed food and had to go.

It took ages to leave. Again I laid hands on the children and then both men and women came seeking prayer. I laid hands on all who came and prayed a blessing. The others had gone.

We left and came back for lunch. It was 4.00pm and we had been expected back by 2.00pm. I enjoyed my food for the first time.

We spent the rest of the day relaxing. David told us that our messages had been powerful and the reference to Ghandi was OK. Leonard had told me he thought it was a mistake, that the man with the microphone had shaken his head. I later found that in India a shake of the head often means 'yes'. I do not know. It is in the Lord's hands.

Tonight two men came to see David, one a businessman trying to sell David some land by the sea, the other the former Principal of a local college which David had once attended and President of the local Gideons. This second man was also father of Franklin, the deaf and dumb member of David's team. He wanted David to build a Christian college. People can see that David is a good man. Franklin's father wanted us to visit his home for lunch or dinner some time.

I had hoped for a call from you, since tomorrow you were going to Scarborough for a few days. I tried to call you but was unable to get through.

Blessing Eight
MONDAY, 17TH NOVEMBER, 1997

The Lembadi Tribe

We awoke to a swarm of flies. There were flies all over our accommodation. There was nothing about to encourage them but the place was full of them. Yesterday I had been preaching about plagues in Egypt. I think it must have been something like this.

We read my Scripture for the day, Romans 8 verses 1-17, and this was quite appropriate for us. Selwyn Hughes commented that one of the most important ministries of the Holy Spirit is to make believers conscious that they are children of God. That spoke to us of our ministry here in India in bringing the good news of Jesus to outcast peoples and bring them into sonship, with all that such a relationship entails.

David came and put some powder about. Eventually the flies started falling and in no time the ants were after them.

At 9.00am we were on the road. Through the busy streets of Chirala we went in a northerly direction and out of town. We passed by a school for deaf and dumb children and a Salvation Army school. We were on our way to a gypsy village three hundred miles into the interior.

David took us to a leper colony at which he had worked for eleven years before setting up his Redemption ministry. When he went there, he took with him medical aid and brought dignity to these people.

When we arrived, people gathered round the jeep and welcomed David with great joy. This was a very moving experience as I looked on men and women with no fingers or toes and clubbed feet. There were many children about. I wept openly as I walked through the village and mingled with the residents. These people are cast-offs from society and are never accepted back into society even when cured. Families live, grow and die in this place. There were lots of little children who were born here and expected to remain here until they die, even though they may never contract leprosy; that is, unless somebody can do something about it. David said that something was being done and he had hope that they would be accepted eventually.

This is at the heart of David Raju's work for the poor and the outcast.

'You have saved my sight. I have no more pain,' one man told David.

We walked on and came to the hospital, both wards full. I put my hands together as a sign of peace and the patients all responded. 'God bless you,' I said. People were eager to meet us and greet us with the sign of peace. It was a privilege to come to this place.

By lunch time we reached Guntur, the main town in the district. Glory, David and Jemima's eldest daughter, was at school here and we visited her. She was fifteen at the time and her sixteenth birthday was just a few days away. She is a lovely girl, quite grown up. We had a brief look around the school and then we left for lunch in a local restaurant.

For lunch we had Indian food, prawns with chicken and fried noodles and coke to drink. This was quite good and we enjoyed it. Then we tried to find a money exchange and some film for Leonard. Even though this is a large town, there are no money changing facilities but we were able to buy some film. We reached Vijayawara, a large city, and on we went. It became dark and we continued until we reached a small village. We were surprised to be able to buy chilled Pepsi so far into the interior. We were going into the heartland of India.

Driving was chaotic even at speed. In one instance I said, 'I thought I needed a toilet but it was OK, I only thought I did!'

At 7.15pm we arrived at Khammam and the Venus Hotel. This hotel seemed of very good quality from the outside. It even had air-conditioning units on the walls. David had booked two rooms for the four of us and all seemed well. The remainder of the team would be sleeping elsewhere. It was disappointing to find that the management had let one of the rooms go because we were later than planned.

We had no time to check our room since we should have been at the gypsy camp by now, and Leonard decided that we would go there immediately after a light meal. We had chicken soup and off we went, straight after that long and bumpy journey. I felt worn out and filthy. It took us the best part of an hour because we were lost down a dirt track and we thought that we would never negotiate the track which eventually led us to the village. Eventually we found the place and the jeep negotiated all the bumps and bends.

Then what a sight! There were more than one thousand people waiting for us and as we arrived on the platform, they garlanded each one of us. What a welcome! There were more than three hundred children squatting in front of us. These were the people of the Lembadi tribe.

Leonard had said that we ought to give a word of testimony and he would speak last. I was asked to start the proceedings. In the rush I had been unable to gather my thoughts. I wasn't really in a state to preach. Please strengthen me Lord for this task You have given me.

I had no greeting in Tilugu since my notes were packed up but I was able to sing *Wakati, Rindu, Moordu* and to encourage the children to sing it. Then I sang *Jesus loves the little children* and the children sang la-las as I sang the words. They loved it and joined in with gusto. It was quite lovely even though flies and other insects were swarming around us in the fluorescent light.

I went on to speak on why I love Jesus:
– for who He is and who I am
– because He came to save me
– because He lives in me
– because He is coming for me
– because He is the same yesterday, today and for ever.

I offered my Saviour to them as the only hope for them and the world.

Robert followed, telling them why Jesus had to go to the Cross and Leonard gave his testimony about how Jesus had lifted him from the pit. He asked people to come forward in faith and there just wasn't room for them all. So Leonard asked them simply to stand. There were hundreds of them. It was an amazing sight. The Holy Spirit had come upon this place in power. We prayed over groups of them and blessed them in Jesus' name. Some true gypsy women, dressed in traditional costume, came, and I prayed with them, laying hands on them. David interpreted my prayers for them.

The people of this village were at one time travellers but had been housed here by the government.

It was now turned 11.30pm and the support team went on to show the Jesus film. It all seemed strange to us, but this was India.

We left after the first spool and reached our hotel at 2.30am. The meeting went on until 4.00am. Some of the team remained in the village to see the film through.

My clothes were filthy and I had been bitten on the hand by mosquitoes. We could find no towels so I dried myself on my shirt. There were only two single beds in our room for the four of us, plus Charlis our driver. Three of us slept on the beds, leaving David and Charlis to sleep on the floor, which they did with no apparent difficulty.

Presenting certificates.

The Redemption logo on the Jeep door.

Residents of the leper colony.

Lembadi children.

Blessing Nine

Our First Baptisms

We rose early this morning. We learned that Dhamaros, the member of David's team we had sent out to prepare for our visit here, originated in this village, Anaypurum. At the time when Dhamaros had joined David's team, David had come here with a view to setting up a Church. We were a part in David's plan and the first to bring the gospel with him.

That mosquito bite was a nasty one. My knuckles were swelling and the wound was weeping. I had never had a bite like that before.

After breakfast in a restaurant, a short walk from our hotel, we set off again for the village, this time in daylight, about forty-five kilometres from Khammam.

The village seemed sleepy today; not surprising since most had been up until 4.00am. Soon they were around us again. The children came singing *'Wakati, Rindu, Moordu'*. I asked David to tell them it was good to see them in daylight, which he did, and they responded that it was good to see us again. I made a handkerchief mouse and let it run up and down my arm, as I have often done with our children and grandchildren. They were really taken with this.

We walked through the village to a place they had arranged and set out chairs for us. They all gathered around and those who had come to be baptised sat down on some mats set out in front of our chairs.

David invited Leonard to speak to them. He taught them that

baptism was an outward and physical sign of an inner and spiritual grace. This was good teaching. To my surprise, I was asked to address them also. I said that the Spirit of God would come upon them and enable them to live the Christian life, serving Him in the world and growing in holiness until they would take on bodies like His glorious body. Robert then followed with words of encouragement.

Then we prepared to go for the baptismal service. The baptismal party squeezed into the back of the jeep, the rest of the team on top. I was glad that we weren't up there. Off we went along the bumpy track to the main road. Along the way we stopped in order to buy a lungi, a robe for Leonard to wear when baptising. We came to a river, a beautiful place, and there Leonard, David and Dhamaros baptised the three women and two men. It was a wonderful moment.

We left those returning to the village at a road junction and we went to our hotel.

After a wash and brush up, we returned to the village. The road seemed to be getting longer and longer each time we travelled along it.

It was about 6.30pm when we arrived and it was already dark. We noticed special posters welcoming us. Children ran up to us singing 'Wakati, Rindu, Moordu'. The jeep went on through the village. It was dark and we could see nothing outside of the glare of the headlights. We stopped and out we got. We went into a field with only a single torch between perhaps a dozen of us. I had sandals and I had no idea what was creeping about. We struggled through a field of maize and eventually reached a Hindu shrine to the rain god. There were cups and plates there on which people left food for the god. There I witnessed the tearing out of a Hindu shrine so that it could be replaced by the worship of the One true God. I found out that there were four villages represented here and they had all accepted Jesus Christ as Lord and Saviour. This was awesome. There must have been over two thousand people converted here.

The strap on my sandal broke whilst walking across the field but I could walk with reasonable ease. We returned to the village. There weren't so many there as last night but it was early.

I was asked to sing before we spoke. I asked the children to sing the song, which they did with gusto. I asked them to promise that they would continue to sing it when we had gone and to tell other boys and girls,

'Jesus loves me,
Jesus loves you.'
They said that they would.

Then I sang *Jesus loves the little children* and David encouraged them to sing la-las to it and clap. The children though it all wonderful. Perhaps they became over-excited as a result of this, for they became difficult to control and were a little noisy. That made it difficult to preach because all the children were under cover and the adults in the open. The noise from the children was contained within the gazebo-like tent.

Robert spoke first on the Beatitudes and the holy life. I had decided to preach on the Treasure and the Pearl and to encourage them to be pearls for Jesus both as individuals and as a community. Leonard preached on ridding themselves of idols and used the story of Dives and Lazarus to illustrate the need to follow Jesus now, and in doing so to leave all else behind.

Anand had a brief word and then David spoke from Isaiah 45 v 16, 'All the makers of idols will be put to shame and disgraced; they will go off into disgrace together.' I didn't understand the words but I felt the power of this man's preaching. If he has anything to do with it, the gods have gone and will remain gone. This village worships the one true God and has no other gods with which to compare Him.

Leonard did the altar call as usual. We had noticed that there was a war being fought tonight. There were many more here but we had each felt it difficult. It seems that Satan didn't like what was going on here but there was no doubt that the victory was the Lord's. There were another twenty or so who came forward tonight. Leonard prayed for them.

Whilst Leonard was preaching tonight, some of the children had come round the side to ask me to make a handkerchief mouse and I had to intimate to them that they should listen to the speaker. Children are the same everywhere but it added to our difficulties.

In spite of these problems, the Church of Jesus Christ is set up here. There will many more baptisms for David to follow up. We agreed to help him provide Bibles and he hoped to establish Dhamaros as their Pastor.

We came away worn out but rejoicing at the power of God shown in this place.

This was not a good place for me in regard to mosquito bites. They attacked me continuously. My right hand had been badly swollen all day and my face looked more like Ursa Major. The bites were big and weeping. I had bites even under my trousers, both back and front and in the middle of my back. It seemed that I was the only one suffering in this way.

Off we went to bed, at least three of us in the two beds. This time it was my turn to sleep without the pillow. David slept on the floor again.

Blessing Ten
WEDNESDAY, 19TH NOVEMBER, 1997

Back to Chirala

Our reading this morning was 1 John 3. What a beginning this chapter has: 'How great is the love the Father has lavished upon us that we should be called children of God!' The commentaries are superb and much appreciated by all of us. The prayer invited us to ask our Father to set our hearts on fire with a new awareness of what it means to belong to Him. O that all Christians would be on fire in the knowledge and love of our Father and in His service! Father, bring that same fire to these people to whom we are bringing the Gospel.

I applied antihistamine cream to my bites and covered myself with repellent, but I felt I was wasting time and effort.

We couldn't even get a cup of tea in the hotel so we walked through the town to a restaurant we found yesterday morning. The team had returned to the village to load the equipment and bring those members who had stayed behind last night. We had water in the restaurant and they brought some dry bread. It seemed that they were unable to make toast. Then they brought some flat omelettes and I ate a little of them. O for some good English food! They then brought some jam in a dish but we insisted on having a jar so they had to go out and buy one.

I asked David about his training background. He had spent two years at Bible College and three months with World Radio in Bexhill, Sussex. He had been seeking ordination through the Church of the Nazarene here in India, but although many promises had been made, nothing much had happened except that he had a one-year license as a Minister. Leonard thought that the Southern Baptists would welcome David into their Ministry. I wondered about the Methodist Church, which supports development by indigenous people. Whatever, we were agreed that the last thing David needs is a hierarchy dictating to him. He does need support though.

We talked about Bibles in Tilugu. Apparently the Gideons have only the New Testament and Psalms. David wants the whole Bible. I could see why he needs that, having heard him preach from Isaiah with such power. Much of the Old Testament speaks against idol worship and that is needed very much in India.

About noon we were ready to set off back to Chirala. At Vijaywara David took us into a restaurant. I could tell as I walked in that this was classy. David said that it had been recommended to him. The room was darkened and air-conditioned and the waiters were dressed properly for the job. We were served with a rather lovely soup and then chicken with noodles and a sweet and sour concoction. This had been prepared by a real professional chef. David was shocked when he received the bill. By our western standards it was reasonable but he said that at that price he could have served a feast at home. Such spending is not for David. Better live simply and let any excess be used for the Lord's work.

At Guntur we dropped off two of the team. They would continue to Chirala by local bus. We were going to collect Glory from school and take her home to celebrate her sixteenth birthday. We found that she had already left school, apparently to go to David's sister's house, also in Guntur. We went there, met David's sister and had tea with her. Glory had returned to Chirala and David was concerned that Glory should do that. Later we found that another member of David's family had taken her.

As we drove through the streets of Guntur, we were involved in an incident which showed how dangerous it is when animals and traffic come together. A cow butted a young girl and threw her under our jeep. How Charlis managed to react as quickly as he did I will never know. She picked herself up, laughed with her friends and walked away.

It was quite late when we arrived back in Chirala but it felt really good to be back home. Jemima had prepared supper. We gave Glory the gifts we had brought from home.

There was a power cut as David switched on the water pump and we sat outside. The phone in David's office rang but David couldn't get the keys in time. I felt sure it was you and I hoped that you would try again later. Later on it rang again and it was indeed you. It was so good to hear you. You sounded so much better, bright and positive. Scarborough and our dear friend Molly were doing you good. Thank you Lord for Molly.

There were letters waiting for me, two from you and one from Emmy and Lily Illingworth for Leonard and me. It was good to read all of them, even though one of yours had been written before we had set off and the other on the morning of our departure.

I managed a shower. I don't think I have ever felt the benefits of a shower quite as much as I did on that occasion. I then wrote a letter to you and went to bed.

Oh, I was glad to be back!

Blessing Eleven

The Fisherfolk Withdraw Their Money

Today we planned to go to the bank to release money to the fisher folk so that they could purchase equipment.

As we woke, the flies were swarming again. We were ready and had the fly killer working. We swept the floor three times before leaving at about 10.00am.

We travelled through villages with broken roads, deep puddles and deep ruts. These roads were never made for the heavy transport that pounds them and they can only get worse. Cattle are led along them to find pasture, which is scarce. I remember thinking that if communities could work together as the fisherfolk are doing, then the cattle could be led to pasture off the roads. David is showing through his work that things can be changed.

After about thirty-five kilometres we arrived at the bank. It is situated on an unmade street in a village. The road was wet and rather deep in mud. Inside the bank David met a man who was President of the men of the fishing village and a lady who presides over the women's group. There were bank books with the photographs of those authorised to withdraw money. There was 63,000 rupees (£1,000) in the men's account and 10,000 rupees (less than £200) in the women's account. The men catch the fish and the women use the money for their own projects. The separate accounts are needed to give the women independence. The money is made up of community savings and a government grant.

David and the man signed the cheques and the lady signed with

her thumb print. David said that he hoped that one day she would
be able to sign it properly when she has learned to read and write.

The men were going to buy fishing nets and they received
bundles of notes. It seemed a fortune. These people have a very
responsible job in handling this amount of cash on behalf of their
community.

Through David I asked them what they thought of the scheme
and they responded that they were very happy about it.

David had hoped that we might be able to meet some of the
fishermen for them to show us their inland fishing scheme, but
there was no-one about.

We drove up to the inland fishing lakes. The fish are stocked in a
rather large old quarry. The nets are designed in such a way that the
small fish escape for another day. There was a small hatchery which
we were not able to see. The whole of the local community depends
on the success of this scheme.

We returned to Chirala. As we travelled through the villages, it
was clear that we were strange creatures to those whom we passed.
Some waved and we waved back. We stopped at one village for a
Pepsi and saw a tractor pulling an image of a Hindu god. David
said that they do this in order to beg. They pretend it is for the
temple but often any gifts offered never arrive there.

There was another letter from you today and it was good to read
it.

Back in our accommodation we cleared out the flies again and
after lunch we rested. Later in the afternoon we were out at the
back of David's house, the first time we had seen this. Robert Old
was repairing the winding mechanisms on the jeep doors. The
electronics had broken down – not surprising in view of the
hammering the jeep takes on the roads, and he was converting it to
manual operation. At least we would be able to open and close the
windows, which until then had not been possible.

The disabled children were there. David and Jemima were caring for them at the back of their home until such time as they could acquire appropriate accommodation for them. David said he thought he would be able to find somewhere within the next week. It was clear that lessons were being provided for the children.

Then off we went to the shops in Chirala to purchase saris. We went to a rather plush-looking shop. They sat us down on a padded floor and showed us all kinds of material. We drank Coke, courtesy of the management. We thought that we would be paying for these gifts for home but they were gifts from our hosts. David did a deal and off we went.

Late on into the evening David came into our room. Leonard went over his thoughts about supporting David in his work and said he thought he could guarantee to raise the money for David to buy the land he wanted to fulfil his vision. I said that I would raise money but at this stage would not put a figure on it. I said that he should be satisfied that his vision was big enough, even if it would take a long time to complete it. I advised that he should think about the long term and ensure that the work could continue in his absence. Leonard again said he thought David would do well within the Baptist Church. I referred to the Baptist hospital at Vellore, where our friends Tony and Judith Sykes are working for the Baptist Missionary Society. I said that I would ring them and ask if a Baptist Missionary was available to come and see David's work or meet us in Madras.

David was very quiet. Hardly a word passed his lips. Perhaps all this was too much at one go. The possibilities are enormous but he needs to operate within his capacity.

It was turned midnight when David left us.

Blessing Twelve

FRIDAY, 21ST NOVEMBER, 1997

The Chinsu Tribe

Today we had intended to set off early but it was Glory's birthday and later today she would be returning to school in Guntur. Mum and Dad rightly had to spend time with Glory on her sixteenth birthday.

The flies were with us again and it was good to leave them behind as we went for breakfast. There we sang 'happy birthday' to Glory. She wants to study medicine. She is a bright and lovely girl. Each of us gave her a small gift.

We waited in our room for most of the morning, preparing for the next few days. Eventually David came with Jemima and Glory. 'Pray for Glory, brothers,' he asked. So we joined hands and one by one we prayed for her. Jemima wiped tears from her eyes. Glory was about to return to school.

At about noon we set off. The jeep was full since on this occasion Jemima came with us. Our direction would be almost due west, right into the interior again. The roads were poor as usual. We passed by women walking towards us. They were earning a pittance working in the tobacco fields.

Eventually we reached Ongole, a large town. Here there was a hotel and David took us there for lunch. The uniformed gentleman on the door saluted us and in we went. There was an air-conditioned room on the fourth floor and we went in for our lunch. David ordered for the five of us. The table only seated four and Jemima sat at an adjacent table. When the food came, there was none for Jemima and as she had ordered something different from us, there was little we could do. We ate our chicken while Jemima waited for her Indian-style food. We also had some fish and noodles.

I was surprised that there was a table where the customers were rather rowdy and a little the worse for drink. I didn't understand the language but I am sure it wasn't fit for anybody, let alone a lady.

Eventually Jemima's lunch arrived and it was enough for four. I am sure that the sight of all that food wasted was upsetting for her.

We told David that there was no need for him to feel that he had to bring us here but we were to return on a few occasions.

On we went along very bumpy and often single-track roads for hours. We reached Gaddalur, a sizeable town, and in the heart of the town we suffered a puncture. This was definitely not a place to have such a mishap. The jeep was jacked up and the wheel taken away to a garage for repair. We were crowded in with people at the windows. We felt rather precarious with the jeep jacked up. I tried to make conversation but it was difficult. I talked about the Indian cricketers and told them that Sachin Tendulkar had played for Yorkshire and that I had seen many of their Test players.

Then Leonard made a mistake. He took out of his pocket five silver American coins and handed them out. Well, every inhabitant of Gaddalur wanted one, even though they were worthless in India, and they pushed up against the jeep causing it to rock. Then the inevitable happened. A man with a little child in a beautiful yellow dress came. He was begging.

The tyre was returned and fitted and we were relieved to be on our way. The sunset was lovely but it was soon dark.

We came to Dornala, where we would be staying the night. It would be about 6.30pm. David booked the rooms. We couldn't see any sign of an hotel.

We carried on and into the tiger reserve, and eventually we

arrived at a white school building. It seemed to be in the middle of nowhere. It was certainly the back of beyond. It was 7.30pm.

We had come to the Chinsu tribe. There were about a hundred children waiting for us but not many adults. Perhaps we were a little early for them. We waited around for a while and then some of our group began singing some of their Tilugu songs, which attracted quite a good congregation.

I was asked to do my bit with the children, which I had become used to doing. They loved it. I told them that the children at home sent their love to them and asked if I could take their love back home. They readily agreed.

I was asked to preach first. I didn't realise the significance of that at the time but this tribe had never heard the gospel of Jesus before and so I was the first person in history to bring the Good News to them. I later found that this had also been the case with the Lembadi tribe. David had asked us to preach the Gospel raw without frills. I spoke of Advent, of Judgement and Resurrection, both in the future and now. Jesus is coming. Now is the time for judgement. There is a resurrection now in the quality of life which Jesus brings, in living like children of the King, in improving their lot for themselves and their children. That is what David and his Redemption team are trying to help them do. I called on them to repent and believe.

Robert spoke on the reason for the Cross and Leonard summed up all that had been said. 'You will know the signs of His coming,' he told them, 'He is coming soon.' Ten people came forward. Some were clearly repenting and crying out for salvation. We prayed with them. There was one man with his wife and a little child. They asked for baptism and we intended that we would perform the ceremony next day. David told us later that he thought he might be able to build a Church on this man. David was disappointed at the turnout but God had done a significant work here tonight.

We had just finished preaching when there was a bright flash across the road and the lights went out. It was the transformer supplying power to the place. There was no hope of that being put right that night. What timing! The Word of God had been proclaimed and the people God was calling had responded.

We returned to Dornala. It was about 10.30pm when we arrived. This is really a backward area. We stepped out of the jeep and across the very muddy street, up a narrow alley and climbed some concrete steps. There were bunks out in the open, packed together and all with bodies on them. We were taken to private 'rooms'. Ours had two single beds and just enough room to stand at the side with both pushed together. We had the luxury of an Indian toilet and a tap. It was so basic and small. Three of us would occupy this room.

We decided that it wasn't worth getting changed for bed, so we slept dressed as we were. We were getting as close as we could to identifying with the people but we were still living in luxury compared to them. If we had slept outside, I might as well have written to the mosquitoes inviting them to have me for supper.

David had chosen this tribe from a survey he had carried out into the places where the Gospel has yet to be proclaimed. He said that one lady had been crying out for salvation, to be accepted into the Kingdom, to be called a child of God. They had never prayed to the one true God before but the words had been pouring out of them as they sought Him. He also said that as this village was in the tiger reserve, sometimes tigers walk down the road.

This is exciting but Chirala is like Paris compared to Dornala.

Blessing Thirteen

A Day with the Chinsu

This is the day that the Lord has made;
We will rejoice and be glad in it!

This was the middle day of our visit to India.
We awoke in our cell. I had felt an uneasy stomach during the night but all was well this morning. We washed with wipes and managed a shave and a clean shirt, but that was it. We were intending to return to Chirala that night and we could manage until then.

David brought us some bread and bananas and later on some toast with our jam and Leonard's peanut butter. There was also some rice and onions. Jemima was preparing breakfast in her cell using a stove she had brought with her. She had realised how difficult it would be to buy food suitable for us and had gone to all this trouble. We also enjoyed a cup of tea. In the circumstances this was wonderful and we were truly grateful.

Outside, below us, was an open sewer with pigs digging their snouts in it. Alongside was the back of a shop where fresh food was being prepared.

There was much hanging around this morning. The team had gone back to the village to prepare for the baptisms and the meeting tonight. The service would start at 8.00pm and the plan was to be back on our way to Chirala by 10.00pm. Knowing what I did about India time, I had my doubts about that, but we lived in hope.

As we waited, we watched a pair of wild monkeys play around on a building opposite. Later they appeared with two little ones and they danced around below us.

David brought us oranges and pomegranates as we waited.

Eventually the boys returned and their report concerning our meeting tonight was good. They said that we had been well received last night. The person seeking baptism had asked to receive further training before baptism and we all agreed that this was wise.

It was noon before we were ready to move, and off we set back into the tiger reserve. It was an opportunity to see the scenery but we saw no tigers. It was hilly country with fields in the large valleys and trees on the hills. We came to an isolated village and had a look around. Most of the residents were out in the fields, so we set off back to the place of our meeting yesterday. We went on to the adjacent village. People live very simply. Some women were cooking outside their huts and then we met some young men with their bows and arrows. The arrows had metal tips. They still hunt with bows and arrows here.

On we went to another village a few miles further along the road and we asked some men if we would be able to tell them about Jesus. They agreed and said they would tell others in the village. There didn't seem to be many coming but the team started singing their Tilugu songs and one by one a crowd gathered. David asked each one of us to speak, me last this time. We all presented the Christian Gospel and David asked how many were interested. Many hands were raised and David promised to follow this up with them.

We returned for the evening meeting. We were early and had to hang around for a while. The meeting began by showing the first spool of the Jesus film. There had been no opportunity to show it the night before due to the power cut. The film was different from the one we had seen before and it seems that there are two versions, one of which, this one, is more faithful to Scripture.

There followed some singing and quite a crowd gathered. There are only about one thousand people in this area, so most of them must have been there. As before, there were many children present.

Robert spoke first and then I. I spoke on 1 John 4 verse 10, 'This is love: not that we loved God, but that He loved us and sent His Son as an atoning sacrifice for our sins.' This was an extension of my testimony. Leonard followed and gave the altar call. I saw eighteen hands raised but then saw others in the darkness, perhaps twenty-five or more altogether. Leonard prayed for them all.

Then we returned to Dornala and the team showed the remaining parts of the film. With members of the team still there, it wouldn't be possible to return to Chirala that night.

The cell didn't seem so bad tonight but I was determined not to make use of that toilet. We slept fully clothed as before.

Our first baptisms.

Jemima, David and Glory.

Chinsu with bow and arrow.

A good catch.

Blessing Fourteen

SUNDAY, 23RD NOVEMBER, 1997

Rapalla

It was raining this morning. Jemima prepared our breakfast again and we were soon ready to set off back home.

We travelled the hundred miles or so to Ongole in heavy rain. The roads were wet, potholed and rather poor.

We just managed to squeeze past a lorry and bus mangled together. It seemed that we were going far too fast but it took four hours to reach Ongole. There we had lunch in the same hotel as before. This time it was quite pleasant. We were the only customers.

We were soon off again and we eventually arrived at a schoolroom in a small village. This village was Rapalla. Here the schoolroom was packed with about one hundred and fifty people, mainly women and children but some men. They were singing lustily following the lead of Jeylekshmi, one of the nurses. We had come to Rapalla to dedicate the Church.

Leonard was asked to speak first. As he rose, somebody asked if the Englishman was going to sing some songs. It seems that my fame had preceded me. After assuring her that I would be singing, all was ready for Leonard to speak.

He based his message on the prayer of Solomon on dedicating the Temple. Leonard said that the Temple of God was within them and they had to build on the firm foundation of Jesus Christ.

I sang the songs as agreed. I had planned to speak on Jesus being given a body but felt the need to change it to the Treasure and

Pearl. I asked them to agree to be God's treasure and pearl, to shine for Jesus, reflecting His glory in their lives, which they did.

Robert concluded the messages, encouraging them as a Church to be a living Temple.

I was last out once again and became hemmed in by people seeking prayer. One lady had brought her own oil for anointing and asked for prayer for the healing of her shoulder. Then another lady borrowed the oil and asked for her shoulder to be anointed. I must have prayed with more than thirty people individually.

We were then invited into the home of one of the members. We sat outside on a kind of patio and were brought bananas, biscuits and tea. This was a lovely Christian family of high-caste Hindu background. The man of the house, now in glory, was converted about fifty years ago and the whole family became Christian. There is a son by the name of Joshua, aged seventeen, who wants to attend Bible School. He will be David's first student. Joshua's sister is also interested. David said that he wanted to train Joshua to be Pastor to this village.

Then we went around to the back of the house, where there was an area of open land. This is the land on which they planned to build a Church for three hundred people. We stood in a circle and Leonard offered prayers for dedication of the land for the glory of God.

On we went to the village school at which Jemima is a teacher. There were boys playing cricket in the field. We joined in and I had to explain to Leonard that he had to keep his arm straight when bowling. I had a ball and with the second ball, hit the wicket. I never expected to be so successful. Oh, I should say that my first effort never reached the other wicket. The ball stuck in my hand and fell out a few paces in front of me to much laughter. It seems I had the last laugh. I also enjoyed a knock.

We met one of Jemima's colleagues. It seems that this school is much regarded in the area.

We then returned to Chirala and I was greeted with the news that you had called earlier whilst we were away. I expect that you would have found that call difficult, with nobody there who could speak English with any fluency. I hoped that you would try again.

I managed to ring Tony and Judith Sykes and make provisional arrangements to meet them in Madras. They said that there were no Baptist Missionary Society people in Vellore save themselves and one other worker. Tony's 'boss' was in Sri Lanka but Tony said that he would be pleased to meet David about his work so that he could pass on the information and perhaps arrange a visit to Chirala.

We went for dinner and as we were eating, you rang. You said that you thought I was cold towards you. It was difficult expressing my feelings with everyone around me. What could I do to comfort you? I was so homesick and was missing you just as much as you missed me. I told you that if I could, I would fly home tomorrow. Then you told me the hospital had asked you to go for an operation two days after my return home and you didn't know what to do. I told you that you needed the operation and that I would be home to be with you. I said the wrong thing and only proved my coldness. What could I do? You said that you had to go for tests before I came home. Please God grant Marion peace. You told me that I could ring Tony but not you and I had to explain yet again that I was unable to make calls out of India, that I depended entirely on you ringing me. What could I do? I felt so helpless and all the time the others could hear what I was saying.

I should have asked you for your measurements for a top for you but in the stress of the situation I forgot.

Blessing Fifteen

David Raju

Today we planned a rest day. The shower this morning was wonderful but there were more mosquito bites. This time there was one on my right cheek, up against my nose, and it was badly swollen. My hands were itching and the left hand swollen.

At 7.00am Eva rang Leonard. Apparently you had been in touch with her and both of you were feeling that time had stood still.

Leonard had a word with David about detailing his plans. David said he would let us have his budgets and a photograph of each child in his care. Leonard presented David with a bundle of travellers cheques to the value of $3,000.

Mr Assirvadam, the former College Principal and President of the local Gideons, called this morning. That night we were going to his home for dinner and Jemima would be going to help prepare the meal.

In the afternoon we conducted an interview with David.

He is the son of Elisha and Emily Raju, both of whom were converted through the ministry of missionaries. Elisha was a male nurse in the missionary hospital and Emily was a teacher. David was born in the American hospital near his home.

In 1977 there was a crusade in Chirala. It was during this crusade that God called David to attend Bible School. Earlier, in the previous year, when a second-year student at university, he had had an opportunity to work among a group of leprosy patients and had felt a call to continue working among them.

So, following his time at Bible School, he went to work in the leper colony, taking with him medicines and drugs. In bringing healing of the body he told them about the Gospel of Jesus Christ. He worked there for eleven years.

He saw an even greater need in the villages and felt restricted in being limited to the leper colony. Accordingly, in 1988 he formed his own organisation, Redemption.

He came to England to be trained at Bexhill in Radio Evangelism. He then went to America to find out how he might help people in India. There he met some people who wanted to help him, including Leonard Nash. He had a vision of a Bible School near Chirala but needed support, which so far had eluded him. He explained his vision to his new friends and was encouraged by their comments and support.

India is a big country with many problems and David says it needs support from wherever it might come. He is working regionally in Andhra Pradesh to help neglected people, meeting not only their physical needs but also their spiritual needs. Indians worship all kinds of gods and there is work to do in presenting the Gospel.

He has a talented and eager young group to support him but even so the workers are few for such a great harvest. He asked us to pray that so many in darkness might receive the Gospel and thereby be brought into the light.

His projects were described as follows:-

The fishermen and their families are tribal, neglected people who need social help and the Gospel. In the early months of his Redemption ministry he pedalled his bicycle around all the villages, talking to the residents about their problems and what they might do about it.

Eventually he was able to put schemes together and receive grants from government and charitable trusts in other countries to fund his social schemes.

He started adult education, the objective being to enable people to read the Bible and build a Church. Instruction is also being given on how to catch fish. David said that the priority is for them to know Christ. They will then take their nets in response. Without Christ they are nothing. With Him they have joy and dignity and a reason to build a better life both for themselves and their children. I can confirm that this was my own experience as I shared conditions with them.

So David went on to develop income generation programmes through the fishing industry, sanitation and water programmes, education for school drop-outs and building of Church communities.

He has brought in good, well-trained staff to manage these schemes and to help him extend the benefits into other communities.

The savings programme is essential since the communities start with nothing with which to purchase nets and fishing boats. The people save a small amount each month and deposit it in a bank account. Then their savings are supplemented by a much larger grant. The savings and grant are then used to buy equipment, say for fifty fishermen, who then put part of their earnings in the account to help finance equipment for the next fifty, and so on until the communities become self-sufficient. This scheme is working in thirty villages and he plans to extend this scheme to the Lembadi and Chinsu tribes in the interior.

The sanitation programme has been applied in all the villages. They now have safe water from wells and the building of toilets and washing facilities is going ahead.

The wells are funded by Water Aid, a British charity. People are given their dignity. The Gospel is preached, Churches and Sunday Schools are set up, and life for these people is turned upside down.

Health education is provided through the three district nurses, who provide medicines and teach public and personal hygiene.

Twenty Churches have been established and these will need the support of the Bible School. David meets people every day who are asking to attend Bible School. Some Church buildings have been built but many congregations are meeting in school buildings, under the trees or in homes. People are poor and contributing to the cost of a Church is difficult if not impossible. Neither are there sufficient shepherds for them.

The missionaries who brought conversion to David's family were Baptists and that could be seen in David's approach.

David has not been ordained, although he has sought ordination. We said we would try to put him in touch with the Baptist Church.

David said that there would be no discrimination in his Bible School. All would be welcome. His plan was to build on the edge of the Bay of Bengal near Chirala. He was negotiating for the purchase of land and hoped to be able to buy it soon. The $3,000 given by Leonard Nash would be invested for that. There was a plot of five acres for sale which would be sufficient for a Bible School, a Church, a home for children and to expand his work.

David has compassion for the neglected people and intends to be in a position to help them.

He wants to build a school for physically handicapped children and drop-outs from school. He has received support from Germany for a scheme to house and educate thirty children. His desire is to enable them to lead a better life, to support them in raising their dignity, and, through vocational guidance, to enable them to be self-reliant. As in other schemes, the overriding objective is to lead them to Jesus. According to the programme, he will have each child for three years.

He is taking the Jesus film to villages and many are coming to faith in Jesus through it.

Blessing Sixteen
Tuesday, 25th November, 1997

Inspected by the Law

This morning started really well; I had an early call from you. It was 4.00am your time and you had been unable to sleep. We were having breakfast and the others left so that we could speak in private. You sounded very calm and confident and we had a lovely conversation. You said that the Depression Group meeting had gone well, with another new member. People at home were excited about what was happening to us here. I told you that I was counting the days to coming home and you said you were thinking about preparing a really good welcome. This time I remembered to ask your measurements but afterwards I realised there was a mistake – your back couldn't possibly be so short!

After breakfast we went to the bank to deposit the American travellers cheques which Leonard had given to David. To do that in Chirala would have taken thirty days and would incur commission charges. We decided that it would be better to sort it out in Madras, where an internal cheque could be made out.

Then we set off towards the sea to have a look at some of the sites available, on which David could build to help fulfil his vision. It had been raining quite heavily overnight and the roads were badly rutted and deep in water.

In Chirala we came upon a large crowd. Apparently someone had died. The body must have been there for some time because there was a strong stench. David later found out that the man had been killed outside the town and his body dumped outside the

Lutheran Church, of which he was a member. The Church people were dealing with his body. It isn't clear how he died.

We passed by the Church we had preached at second on our first Sunday there and then a Hindu temple, at which there was a crowd offering a chicken to their god. We then went past the first Church at which we had preached and on to the beach. There were some fishermen out at sea. On the shore there were some partly constructed buildings and fish tanks. This had been a business venture which had not yet succeeded and they were selling it off in its present form. David said that he thought the asking price was too high and that it would be better to find a virgin site on which to build for the vision. We went back inland to see three more sites, all of them within sight and walking distance of the sea.

We went to see a local fisherman who knew something about the land. He wasn't at home so we went into the village to look for him. There we enjoyed a Pepsi and as we did so, some fishermen came past us carrying their catch in a big net. It seemed to be a good catch.

David found the fisherman we were looking for and he returned with us to the three plots. It was clear that the land was low-lying and would require considerable earthworks to raise the site levels. Nevertheless David asked the fisherman to negotiate prices and to let him know the outcome. Leonard prayed over the land claiming it for the Lord's work and praying that God would have His way with it.

There was a school nearby built and run by Christians. It was lunchtime and and all the children came out into the fields to do their ablutions. They were out there in full view of everybody, both boys and girls. We came to the first Church we had preached in, which was nearby. Some of the members saw us and brought us Cokes to drink. They were glad to see us and welcome us. Children from the school gathered round our jeep. It was unusual to see white men and they were curious.

When we returned to Chirala, there was a message that the police were coming this afternoon. We wondered what we had done to warrant a visit from the police. David said that they might want to speak to us but not to worry because the Lord would surely take care of us. We waited in our accommodation.

Eventually David came into our room with a tall, dark and impressive-looking gentleman, a senior police officer from Hyderabad. We were introduced to him as David's guests and David went on to show the visitor photographs of his work, which were set out around the walls of our room. Then they left.

After some time David returned. The officer had been through David's books and had talked to him about the office, which had only been constructed about a year before, and about David's work. He told David that the work he was doing was excellent and, almost prophetically, that David would do even greater works than these. This policeman was a Hindu and some of that came out as he told David this was a good place to build an office and that he had a good face, which said that he was enjoying his work. David told him that this was the Lord's work and he always enjoyed being a part of it. The officer asked David if he went to Church. 'Yes,' said David, 'I am a Christian and this is the Lord's work.' 'God bless you,' said the officer. He then asked David to show him his palm but David refused.

David had offered to let the officer speak to us, but he declined, saying that we were visitors and he didn't want to involve us.

David asked if someone had reported our presence and the officer smiled without commenting, an indication that someone had done so.

The officer had indicated that they had considered sending a team of officers, but that he had decided to come himself. It seems that he had been to some of the villages in which David is working and every person he had spoken to had said how much they love this man and respect him.

This afternoon it was heavy and close. The flies were swarming outside and we were only relatively free from them inside. It was stifling with the windows closed.

At 6.00pm David came to take us off to more remote villages. We travelled along narrow, wet and muddy lanes, bumping and turning in the darkness. We reached a fishing village and dropped off two members of the team for them to arrange a meeting later in the evening. On and on we went until we arrived at the home of a fishing family. They brought chairs out for us to sit on under the palm trees whilst they arranged a plastic sheet for people to sit on. Fluorescent lighting was provided, linked to the house electricity. Slowly a crowd gathered. They started singing Tilugu songs and the service had started. As they sang, more and more people arrived until there were perhaps one hundred and fifty there, including the children.

I started with the now customary singing, eventually giving way to Robert who spoke, appropriately, on Jesus the Light of the World. I then followed with my testimony based on 1 John 4 verse 19, 'We love because He first loved us,' and Leonard addressed them on living the Christian life. He asked those who wanted to commit themselves to Jesus to stand, and too many to count did so. Leonard prayed with them the prayer of commitment and afterwards prayed with individuals who came. This was a thrilling experience.

They offered us coconuts but David asked if they minded if we didn't have them now but took them back whole to enjoy later.

We returned to the village at which we had left the two members of the team. They were showing the Jesus film and were almost at the end of the second spool, the point at which Jesus and His disciples had arrived at Gethsemane. The projection of the film was across the main track through the village and there were about fifty people watching.

We waited for the conclusion of the film, which provided a

fitting base on which we could speak. Robert spoke briefly on the truth of which the film spoke. I followed by explaining who it was who hung on that Cross and what He was doing there. Leonard summarised and asked people to stand in commitment, saying the prayer with the twenty or so who stood. He again prayed with individuals who came forward. There was an eighty-year-old man who gave his life to the Lord Jesus Christ and asked for prayer for his sick wife. We noticed that Subaru, a Hindu, prayed aloud the prayer of commitment. Praise God!

It was midnight before we returned to Chirala but Jemima had prepared supper for us. She said that you had called at about 10.00pm and I wondered why so soon after your earlier call.

Blessing Seventeen

Nets for the Fishermen

I reflected that this time next week we would be back in Madras preparing to return home. Meanwhile, the reality was that we were inundated with flies.

The Scripture reading this morning was 2 Timothy 1 verses 1-14 and the heading of the commentary was 'Sewage Treatment'. It really spoke to our situation and experience today.

At 10.30am we were on the road again. We were on our way to present nets to the fishermen. This was a long trip, about two hours, mainly along rough, potholed dirt tracks. Driving along these roads shook us about and was very tiring. Before he had the jeep, David had to visit these villages by bicycle and often arrived home in the early hours. This journey seemed endless, not helped by having to wait for some time at a level crossing. They shut the gates up to half an hour before the train arrives and this is the main east coast line, so the gates are shut for much of the day.

Eventually we arrived at the village and soon people gathered at the central meeting point. These people are immigrants from Tamil Nadu in the south and speak both Tamil and Tilugu.

The men brought sacks of fishing nets out of a building. These nets had been purchased with the money we had seen withdrawn from the bank earlier. They took some nets out of the sacks and made an instant display. We were then invited to present the nets to the fishermen. It was a real honour to be asked to do this. People are at a very base level here, some of the men having the barest cover, simply a loin cloth.

Following the presentation, there was much rejoicing and dancing. The men joined the children in tribal dancing. It reminded me of the many African films we have seen over the years. Sometimes the dancing and chanting became quite intense. As I watched and listened, I wondered how it was that God should bring me to this place in His service.

This village is totally Hindu but there were no Hindu rites in their celebrations, although a Hindu priest was there in the background.

We walked down to the sea shore to see the fishing boats. These were basically banana-shaped laths of wood tied together with rope and were fitted with an outboard motor. We saw some fishermen emptying their nets. These fish were fairly small. They gut them and dry them in the sun. We saw some being dried. There were flies all over them.

The whole village depends on fishing but at present it needs a middleman to market them and the price they get is small. David is trying to help them cut out the middleman.

At about 2.00pm we left along the same dirt track as we had come along earlier and at about 4.00pm we arrived in Ongole for our lunch. It was overfacing, although the chicken soup and noodle dish were good. Both Leonard and I felt nauseated and Leonard brought his back later.

We went to the railway station to reserve seats for the journey back to Madras. David was some considerable time in the booking office and whilst he was there, David's brother-in-law recognised the jeep. David's mother-in-law had been taken into Ongole hospital with chest pains. David returned having tried to book seats but confirmation of his request would be needed later. Then we set off to the hospital. When we arrived, the doctors had done their tests and the results were awaited. Not long after we arrived, the power failed and for a time we were in complete darkness. Eventually the generator was started and the diesel flames floated by us as we waited.

Two of Jemima's sisters were there with their mother and they went with David to see the doctor for the results of the tests. He told them she would be OK but needed rest. David decided that she should come back to Chirala with us so that Jemima could look after her mother. That was in addition to looking after us and those little children.

So we set off back to Chirala with David's mother-in-law and one of Jemima's sisters, who was coming to help Jemima. At a quiet spot we stopped and each one of us prayed for Jemima's mother. It was like Jesus visiting Peter's mother-in-law in Capernaum.

Charlis drove very carefully and the journey back to Chirala seemed to take an eternity. We were very tired and my stomach was still upset following our lunch. Though we asked for no food, some was brought but I was not for eating and went to sleep.

Blessing Eighteen
THURSDAY, 27TH NOVEMBER, 1997
Thanksgiving Day

This was a special day for Leonard and Robert. Back home they would have been enjoying a feast with turkey and all the trimmings.

As usual they were up and dressed before me. When I came out of the shower, David was in our room talking to two businessmen about the site with the part-constructed buildings by the sea. They had originally asked for forty laks rupees (£70,000) but had now reduced the price to fifteen laks rupees and David was negotiating to get the price down to ten laks rupees (less than £20,000). Both Leonard and Robert said that this was a good site but I still had my reservations and had advised to keep options open for as long as possible, at least until the time that David felt in his own heart that this was what God wanted. This site was small, built for the fishing business and not a Bible School, and I still thought it might be better to build on a virgin site. Of course, as I have said, it had nothing to do with us. David had to be sure himself.

When the visitors had left, negotiations still incomplete, David received a message concerning the plot of land I favoured. They had seen us Westerners and had put the price up. They must have thought that we had the money to buy the land. I was certain that David would do what was right.

We were advised to rest for the remainder of the morning. I had received three letters from you written on 13th, 15th and 18th November. It was good to read them.

We managed to see some of Leonard's videos on the TV. These shots were excellent. Subaru brought his video camera and showed some of his film. He had recorded our whole visit and the pictures were superb. David said that we could have copies. That is wonderful.

At about 11.00am David came and announced that we were going shopping. We went into Chirala and went to a men's wear shop. There had been no indication as to what this was all about. He was looking for lalchi and pyjamas (trousers), traditional Indian wear. We were invited to choose material from which to make clothing for each one of us as a gift from David. Then we went to see the tailor about having the material made up. David wanted these to be rather special, to be embroidered, and that needed someone apart from the tailor who had special embroidery skills. We waited with our customary Pepsi whilst all this was sorted out. The embroiderer was overworked and was unable to accept the job, so we would have to find someone else. Our measurements were taken and the embroidery would be sorted out later.

We returned to Baerpet in two rickshaws and that was an interesting experience, the poor driver having to push us for part of the way since his legs were inadequate to pedal us.

After lunch we set off in the jeep back to the Bay of Bengal. There were people there to open up buildings for us so that we could inspect them. There was no doubt that some of the buildings could be modified for use as a Bible School and other buildings for use for the children, although there was no room on that site for expansion. Its greatest asset was the foundations, which were there for all the buildings that would he needed and these foundations had already withstood a cyclone in 1996. David would be able to make a start with minimum construction costs and it was sited right alongside the beach, a prime position.

I found myself singing:

The foolish man built his house upon the sand
The wise man built his house upon the rock

It seems that these foundations are soundly constructed but I was sure that David would have them checked out.

After dinner at 7.00pm we set out for another village north of Chirala. This was along a relatively good road and we arrived shortly after 8.00pm. There was a gazebo, the floor covered and the welcome signs out for us. There were hardly any people there, just a few children. The team began singing Tilugu songs and we sat and waited for the people to come. We waited for an hour and a half, during which time people arrived in dribs and drabs. I had noticed that the building alongside us had a foundation stone dated 1890 and bore the name of an American. I asked David if this was a Church and he confirmed that it was. We could hear singing from another meeting. David said that this was another Christian group who had heard that we were coming tonight. That sounds normal.

Eventually we started and they garlanded us. Many had come with their Bibles, since this was a mainly Christian gathering.

I was asked to sing, which I did, but when I asked people to join in or simply to sing la-las, they kept silent. This was so different from our experiences elsewhere. As I was singing, I swallowed a fly or something and for a while my voice wouldn't function. I think they understood I had met a stranger and let him in, but they didn't sing to make up for my loss.

I was asked to speak first, my voice having returned. Fatigue was starting to set in and I was glad that I had taken the opportunity of the time available today to rest. I decided to give my testimony. It seemed to me that it was the most significant thing I could do. Robert followed with a text from Colossians 1 verses 9 and 10 and he reiterated a point I had made, namely the Christian's responsibility to commend the Saviour to others continually. Leonard came last and pulled it all together.

Tonight it seemed strange. There wasn't the freedom in any of us. This was a Brethren fellowship, in which women had to keep silence. It seemed to us to be an excuse for male domination and we felt very unhappy about it. Christian people often disappoint. I am sure that Jesus never expected women to keep quiet. Women were among his bravest supporters.

In his address Robert had asked for a show of hands to indicate how many had given their lives to the Lord. Almost everybody raised their hands. When Leonard asked if anybody needed special prayers, it seemed that nobody did. It seemed to us that these people had received an inoculation against getting Christianity badly. O for the Holy Spirit to fall on inoculated Christians!

We were taken into another building and sat down before bowls of fruit. They wanted us to feel welcome. It all seemed strange.

I had forgotten one point: the leaders had visited us earlier on our visit to check out our theology. It must have been OK, because they invited us to come tonight.

Blessing Nineteen

FRIDAY, 28TH NOVEMBER, 1997

The Youth Conference

This morning David had heard further from the businessmen concerning the land and buildings by the sea. They had asked to come and negotiate further but he had told them that ten laks rupees was his limit. We gathered in a circle and Leonard prayed that God's will would be done.

We shared together my reading for the day, Ephesians 6 verses 1-9: 'Fathers do not exasperate your children; instead bring them up in the training and instruction of the Lord.' That is what we have tried to do with our children and as I thought about it, I thought how proud I am of them. They are a real treasure. Then there was a prayer which says, 'The best of fathers is but a faint reflection of You.' How true, but how great is His grace that enables us to bring up our children! I thought of my dad and of his struggle over his final months, of his stay in care following his stroke. I felt thankful for my parents as you are thankful for yours.

You rang before breakfast this morning, 3.40am, your time. You were unable to sleep. We chatted for a while. Next Friday we would be together again. You had thought of cancelling our planned trip to see *Les Misérables* in Manchester the day after my return, but I told you I was looking forward to going with you. You said that our little granddaughter Hannah, aged eleven months, had written to me but as yet I had not received it.

Leonard gave me some advice, to make sure my listeners understood just how much Jesus loved them as well as me.

Then David came with Hannah's letter, which Suzanne had written for her. It was so funny. I showed it to the others.

David had received some letters, one from AFPRO (Action for Food Production) asking his views concerning cyclone warning systems and his experiences in giving aid following the cyclone of 1996. There was also a letter from CRY concerning education for all children in India, asking him to support a campaign to ensure legislation is introduced.

This morning we were planned to speak at a Youth Conference in Chirala. We were ready at the planned time of 11.00am but as usual they were not ready. David said that they would come and tell us when they were ready for us. So we spent some time looking at Subaru's video recordings of our visit.

At 12.00 noon the young people came for us and we walked across the main road to the Lutheran Church where they were holding their meetings. This was a good building with seating for three hundred or more but there were no people there. The place was empty. As we waited, young adults came in dribs and drabs until there were perhaps forty or so sitting in the back rows of the Church. We had the feeling that there was not much commitment here.

I was introduced as chief guest, Robert as the speaker and Leonard as 'comments' or something similar. Robert spoke first on Romans 12 verses 1 and 2 about keeping their bodies holy. I followed with my testimony, telling them that Jesus loved them as well and sought a response from them to give themselves into His service.

The Christian Gospel depended on them. Leonard spoke about giants, based on David and Goliath, and how giants in life can be overcome in Jesus. This was tough since there was no life. We were invited to return in the evening but Leonard said that if we did, it would be to respond to their questions. There had to be some input from them.

David was of the opinion that these were Christians in name only, there was no commitment. The most disappointing times had been with so-called Christians.

The rest of the day we spent in our rooms, partly resting and partly watching Subaru's videos of our visit. It was good to be reminded of some of our experiences. I was reminded of a book on our shelves at home, *Blessings out of Buffetings* by Alan Redpath on 2 Corinthians. We had truly been blessed through our buffetings. I felt that we had been lifted on the prayers of the people back home. It was strange watching myself on the TV screen and listening to my stammering tongue singing '*Wakati, Rindu, Moordu...*'

We did not return to the Youth Conference tonight and I was glad of that.

I rang Tony and Judith Sykes. They had arranged to arrive in Madras by about 7.00pm on Wednesday and stay overnight at the YWCA. Tony was having a day's holiday and Judith hoped to do some shopping. There would not be much time to talk to Leonard and Robert but there would be time on Thursday for a long discussion with David and myself.

Blessing Twenty

Muslim Girls and Shepherds

At 10.45 this morning we were on the road again. This time we were journeying south towards Ongole. It was the Saturday market in the first village but beyond there the road was quiet and the countryside was lovely. We looked over green fields and, as it had been raining heavily overnight, there was plenty of water about. The streams were full and overflowing into the rice paddies. We noticed a Christian graveyard almost totally submerged.

This journey was so different from all the others over the weeks. We reached a river in flood. A cyclist was pushing his bicycle across the river and he was knee-deep in water. It reminded me of Ezekiel's vision of the river flowing from the Temple into the Dead Sea and bringing life wherever it flowed. Here the river was knee-deep but throughout this visit we had been way out of our depth in the hands of the Saviour. Glory to Him for bringing us here, sharing in both His sufferings and His glory.

We drove through the water and Charlis tested the brakes. We were on our way again.

It was turned noon when we arrived at the Muslim community in Ongole. Here David had set up a school for Muslim girls. At the time of our arrival they had gone for lunch, so we arranged to return later.

We had lunch at the same hotel as before, soup and fried chicken, quite pleasant.

We called at the railway station to confirm our reservations.

David was told that two seats had been confirmed, which was no good for us, but that was the situation.

We returned to the Muslim village. This was unhygienic, with open drains on both sides of the street and pigs with their snouts in them. David said that this was often the case in Muslim villages but not in Hindu villages, which were generally more tidy.

We went up the outside stairs to a schoolroom and we sat down in a little space in front of a class of twenty-five girls. I asked them if they were learning to speak English and one or two could speak a few words. They said they also learned mathematics and science. Leonard encouraged them in their studies and advised them to learn to speak English, a vital language. They showed us some of their skills on a black drape and then some of their sewing skills. They would be taking exams in March, which, if they passed, would equip them for good jobs.

We found that two of these 'girls' were married. One of the problems of poverty is that young girls are married off at the earliest opportunity. It is tragic. The girls have no say at all in the matter.

The wonderful thing about this school is that Muslim men do not take kindly to women being educated, but they knew of David Raju and his work and had agreed to go ahead on the understanding that he would be in charge of it.

This school is called the 'Dianne Casteel School', after the American woman who sent some money to help provide it. David also has a government grant. When he went to see the local government official for release of the money, the official demanded a bribe. This is standard practice in India. It seems to me an extension of the Hindu religion, which seeks to bribe gods by giving gifts. David had refused to give any bribe on the basis that it was taking money from the children and the one God was against such practice. He wrote to Central Government to complain and eventually the full sum was released.

Off we went to another village, a Hindu inland fishing

community. Here we saw a sanitation programme sponsored by Water Aid, a British charity. Toilet and bathing units were being constructed for each household. We have regularly passed by people using grass verges as toilets, crouching as they do what they have to do. In this village we saw a shower unit rather like the one used by Mitzi Gaynor in the film *South Pacific*. This one was totally see-through – no privacy whatever. The scheme we saw is providing privacy as well as sanitation for all households.

The toilets are Indian-style, a hole in the floor but the contents are piped out of the building into an underground container which drains naturally and collects the solids. These will be emptied out every ten years or so for fertiliser.

They are considerably better than the dry toilets we had seen in many places, particularly in the countryside, until fairly recently.

On our way back to Chirala we called at a shepherds' village on the possibility that we might he able to bring the Gospel. The working people had yet to return so we would have to come back later. Instead, David took us to visit a sick child whose mother had died in childbirth. This little boy had been ill for some time, in and out of hospital. David thought he had been given too much medicine. Each of us prayed over the lad, seeking his full restoration to health and strength. It was another moving experience.

We arranged to return tonight to bring the Word of God.

We had intended to return at 6.00pm and we were ready to go, but David's brother Robert had arranged dinner for us and as he had to catch a train at 10.00pm, there was no way that dinner would wait. We waited for dinner for some considerable time but when it came, it was very good and they had gone to a great deal of trouble.

Due to this delay, it would be 8.30pm at the earliest when we arrived back at the village.

There was nobody at all waiting for us but two members of the team sang the songs and people came. This is a shepherd village.

They shepherd goats. As usual, we had to wait some time before a suitable number turned up, eventually reaching eighty or so.

I did my bit with the children. At last it was beginning to trip off the tongue easily. Then I went straight in to preach on John 3 verse 16.

God. Who? The One true God.
  All others made by man or in the mind.
so loved the world   – even this village
That He gave   – not bought
                    – not bribed
                    – not through chicken offerings
His only Son   – Himself!
so that whoever   – each and every one here
might not die   – the alternative
but have eternal life – the prize!

I had just asked them to decide when we noticed a fire under the jeep and somebody doused the flames. What was happening? It was a little frightening but we settled down and Robert spoke briefly, followed by Leonard on the Good Shepherd.

One man committed himself to Christ. He had until now been attending the mosque. This was wonderful. Almost everybody present raised their hands to show their faith in Jesus. Afterwards we prayed with individuals for blessing and healing. For the first time I was asked to pray for a cow which wasn't producing milk. The lady had brought oil for me to anoint the animal. David explained to me what she was asking and advised me to pray for the cow where we were, which I did, and she was delighted.

David said that the fire under the jeep had been started deliberately, probably by a believing Hindu. My preaching must have disturbed him. Perhaps he sold chickens. Later we noticed that there were no burn marks on the jeep.

There was no Church building here nor any pastor to shepherd the people and they asked us to pray for them as a community. This was a lovely new Christian group.

We returned home. Again, it was after midnight.

Blessing Twenty-One

Preaching in Church and Open Air

This morning we were due at the Lutheran Church at 8.30am. We were ready for breakfast by 7.30am but there is no rush in India. David said there was no chance of them being ready by 8.30am, so we had a leisurely breakfast and wandered across to the Church at about 8.50am. The minister welcomed us and we sat in the front row. He said that the service would start at 9.00am and that the young people would be there. A cut-out sign above the altar told us that this was 'Youth Sunday'. We were invited to sit in the altar area so we took off our shoes and went there.

The service began at 9.30am. It was liturgical, traditional C of E, all prayers sung. They sang the Tilugu version of 'Holy, holy, holy' but we were unable to join in. We were then invited to address the congregation. Robert spoke on the passage from Revelation 3 verses 14ff. about lukewarmness in The Church and the need to become alive in the Spirit.

I decided that I would like to worship God in my own tongue so I sang, 'This, this is the God we adore,' as a solo. I had decided to base my message on Jesus in Gethsemane and our experiences in India, what we had seen and the task facing Christians in this great country. We had seen hopelessness, stared it in the face, not helped at all by the iniquitous caste system which still operated in India, but we had been with Christian people who were doing something about it, struggling to overcome the poverty and to build up the Church. I referred to Jesus and how He came through Gethsemane in obedience to the victory of the Cross. He cried out from the Cross, 'It is finished.' It was finished; He had finished the work God had given Him to do and Resurrection followed, God's Amen to the finished work of Jesus. Christians have crosses to bear here. If Christians don't do anything about it, nobody else will. I called them to be faithful to their calling.

Leonard spoke at length in praise of David Raju. I thought that this must have been difficult for David, since he was doing the interpretation and Leonard had asked him to interpret accurately. Leonard went on for twenty minutes. This left me unhappy. I have difficulty in hearing the praises of people in worship. For me it is vital that we are clear about Whom we have come to worship. I can remember having to plan a service as part of my Local Preacher course on the life of John Wesley. At the time I was very unhappy about it and told my assessor so. It was one of the few 'A' grades I had.

Leonard followed by preaching on the Scripture, for which I was grateful. He said the end times were near and we needed to act accordingly.

There were several scholarly people present, who had good jobs with comfortable living standards. Some thanked me for the challenge. I pray that they will take it seriously. Someone thanked Leonard for talking of David Raju as he did. David was brought up in this community. I hope that they will support David in his work.

David told us that he thought it was OK to speak of him and his work on the grounds that they needed to know what was happening. He also told us that the caste system operates in Christian circles. Perhaps I had challenged them on that.

Afterwards I told Leonard of my difficulty concerning his preaching and he said he was very happy about what he had said. I told him that was OK, I loved him. We see things differently but we set that aside for the good of the Gospel and we thanked God.

In the afternoon we set off towards Ongole to one of the remote villages. We had passed by earlier and on that occasion had seen an outline of a new Church building which was yet to be constructed. Now the roof had been thatched and plastic sheeting fitted around the 'walls'. We had come to dedicate this new Church.

There was a good crowd here waiting for us, about fifty or sixty. We met the lady who had given the land. Leonard had earlier sent some money to cover the cost of materials.

The service of celebration was held outside in the sunshine. They sang Tilugu songs and I prayed. I was then asked to sing for the children and to preach. I preached again on the Treasure and the Pearl. It fits situations like this, especially when it comes to asking them to be pearls, to shine for Jesus, to which they all agreed with some enthusiasm.

Robert encouraged them and Leonard rounded it off.

Leonard then named the Church 'Love and Truth', the name of a Church near his home in Tennessee. He then officially opened the Church and cut the tape. The people were delighted. Refreshments were served and we were garlanded yet again. The lady who had given the land insisted that we have a biscuit, putting one into each mouth. It was lovely to be here.

We went on elsewhere to conduct baptisms. On our way we collected those seeking baptism and on we went to a lake. Cows cool off here but David, Leonard and the two ladies sallied into the water. Baptism was by total immersion and it seemed that the ladies had never had the experience of putting their heads below water, but they rose very happy. The Christian names given to the ladies were Ruth and Deborah.

It was after 8.00pm when we returned to Chirala. At that time we thought that we would not leave until we went for the train on Tuesday.

Leonard went straight for the shower.

Presenting fishing equipment.

Judith with Church members.

Tony and Judith present nets and containers.

Disabled children at lunch.

Blessing Twenty-Two

MONDAY, 1ST DECEMBER. 1997

The Redemption Meeting

It's December! Praise the Lord! Both Leonard and Robert had calls early this morning and were encouraged by them. Then you rang at 9.00am just as we were starting breakfast. It was lovely to hear from you again. What had I been eating? Would roast beef and Yorkshire pudding be OK when I came home? Our granddaughter, Hannah, was climbing stairs and taking books off shelves. You were having tests tomorrow in preparation for your operation, 7.00pm our time. I promised that I would think of you at that time.

You said you were getting used to being alone and I told you not to get too used to it because I was coming home. You talked about a red carpet and I wondered what you had up your sleeve for my return. I said the first thing I wanted was a deep bath and you said 'All is prepared.' I said that I would ring you from Madras.

Leonard had intended to give out biros to the Redemption team. These biros had business addresses on them and David suggested that they should not be widely circulated, as in the wrong hands they might cause letters to be written either begging or defaming his work. Leonard agreed that they would be used in the school.

David referred to a pastor's daughter living nearby who had been complaining that David was keeping young men at his home. He told her she had no need to worry because these young men were born again. 'But I have a daughter,' she argued. 'I have two daughters, but I have no cause for concern,' David replied. There is much jealousy here concerning David and his work. This 'Christian' neighbour had upset Pradesh, David's son, by calling him a 'cobbler's son', one of the lowest caste. David had told him not to concern himself with the things of the world.

I am shocked that so-called Christian people can even countenance the caste system.

The Lutheran Church was considering letting David have part of their premises for his outcast children. This was wonderful. Maybe what Leonard said yesterday had produced the desired effect. Whatever, God would have the glory.

The team came into our room, which we had cleared for the purpose, and Leonard commenced proceedings with prayer.

It was reported that Rahill, the lady who had given the land for the Church we dedicated the day before, asked if anything could be done for the elderly residents of the village who could not be cared for by their children. This was a good example of concerns being identified by the people. Apparently many elderly people have to try and keep working in rice paddies long after they should have retired, just in order to live. This could be an extension of Christian social activities.

Leonard was invited to speak to the meeting. He encouraged them to be faithful to their leader, David. He expressed his appreciation of their work and asked them to stick together, to share the same vision and to stick to the plan. The disciples of Jesus had shown jealousy and it could come even here. If it did, they must not let it destroy them but overcome it. David commented that in the communities there are wolves among the sheep and they needed to be 'gentle as doves but wise as serpents'. There will always be those who want to make something out of their work. Leonard went on to ask them to do what they could with the gifts that they had but to expect far more from God. They should get more training, learn to become better at what they do. He said that after this experience he would never be the same again and he gave thanks to God for them. They were the Good Samaritan, children of God, children of the King, not measured in castes; that is what they are.

Robert said that there was a drawback. There simply weren't enough of them for all the work that was needed but they should pursue the vision. Everything they were enabled to do was a gift from God.

There was discussion on the documentation work undertaken by Subaru. David said that they needed a brochure about their work and Robert had agreed to produce one for them. Robert said that Subaru should continually strive to improve his understanding of English and the computer. He advised the meeting that projects should be separately documented.

At this point David took a telephone call from the businessmen concerning the plot of land by the sea. They agreed to sell at ten laks rupees, the very price David was holding out for. Halleluia!

Subaru gave his testimony concerning his time with Redemption, referring to the good work which was being done and his introduction to the Word of God. He said that he is at peace here. It was lovely to listen to him.

Anurpurna, one of the ladies, confirmed that women generally were uncomfortable at coping with their ablutions without privacy, and were delighted at the hope of having toilets and shower blocks. I said that I would write to Water Aid about that.

During our lunch break we met Charlis' brother. He had a high fever. I have never touched anybody so hot before. Leonard anointed him with oil and we all prayed over him. Since their father died, their mother had been staying with her brother and the two lads had been staying here. It is these young men that the neighbour had been complaining about. Charlis' brother had medicine and had to rest until the fever subsided.

In the afternoon we sat in a circle outside in the sunshine as each member of the team went through their particular programme for the coming week. This was really businesslike.

David went through his overall vision for Redemption and this led to a discussion on the elderly abused.

Anand said that the elderly have wisdom but are neglected. In India there is no social security and old people are often thrown out of the home, which leads to begging. They should be kept at home with food and shelter. Serath said that in India, when the oxen become too old, the butcher sees them off. People are treated like oxen. (I think they are often treated worse than animals!). A home is needed to give them hope. Solomon said that nobody seems to care. It isn't enough simply to talk to them, they needed shelter. Anurpurna added that if the elderly have money, they will be cared for, but if not, the attitude is not good although there are exceptions. Mamoharama said that it is like this: someone may have four sons with daughters-in-law. The eldest son may say that they can't cope with Mother and all the others say the same so it ends up like a game with Mother in the middle. Bhaghyavathi said that some elderly people don't want to bother their children and work on in the rice fields and live lives of very hard suffering. Krupa added that some old people have no children at all and worry about who will care for them when they become too old to look after themselves. Salman said that costs were increasing and more people were caught in the poverty trap. It was difficult to feed all the old people.

David summed up by saying that being old was a curse when it ought to be a blessing. They should have time to study, to worship and to help in the community. They have wisdom and considerable potential. A 'Help the Aged' programme is needed. He proposed that children should contribute to the care of the elderly and a fund should be started under the control of a committee in each village. The elderly could do things like cultivating kitchen gardens, looking after and teaching children, looking after those elderly people weaker than themselves.

It was agreed unanimously that action should be taken.

So, the meeting continued, covering the various areas of activity.

Day Care Centres. Solomon referred to the work of David's brother Robert, but said that the Government isn't dealing with everybody in providing nutrition and supplementary feeding. They tend to support those who support them in elections. Serath said that these were for the neglected people. He would like to see programmes in slums where people are malnourished and need Christian education.

David concluded that this could be merged with a programme for the elderly in which the old people can play a part. All agreed.

Shelter for the Homeless. Serath began by referring to the problems caused by cyclones along the coast. Many people are made homeless. The government grant for rehousing was 12,000 rupees (£200), which had to cover the cost of building and was nowhere near enough. David's scheme involves contributions from those displaced, even if only in the form of labour, the value of which he can recover.

So David encourages them to be rehoused and this is another reason for people believing in the One God and building Churches.

Church Plantation. Serath said that people in most villages were looking for a building in which to worship. Sometimes they use a local school, but often the government agency refuses to let it and worship has to take place under trees or in a house. A simple building is adequate. Other activities could take place in the Church, such as youth work, Bible teaching, keyboard instruction, use of PA systems, literature distribution and Sunday school work. He said he thought that another jeep was needed simply for outreach work.

Bible School. The vision was to bring in people from the villages to train as pastors and leaders and for it to be inter-denominational. The whole team shares this vision and so do we, their visitors.

Film Ministry. They are seeking to develop their own team. They enjoy good support from Campus Crusade for Christ but are able only to show the Jesus film and the opportunities are limited. They are looking to provide their own ministry.

Radio Ministry. This would reach all homes, even Muslim homes, and the impact would be powerful.

Pastoral Support. They are looking to provide financial support for their pastors rather than other people thinking they are only wanting worshippers for their money.

Sunday School Support. There is no literature, music, visual aids etc. Sunday school needs to be bright and properly run.

Bible Printing. They want the whole Bible to be available to all at minimum cost and this would be provided by having their own press.

After all that, I gave my valedictory address, summing up all that we had seen in India, rather like the summary I did for you at the beginning of this letter. I am adding a section at the end to record it for you.

One by one they spoke of their gratitude for our visit, of the assurance of their prayers for us for safe journeys home, and their hope that we would all return. It was another lovely experience.

We presented each member with a document case and then Leonard closed the meeting with prayer.

Subaru arrived with our lalchis. They were lovely and we all thanked David for them.

Blessing Twenty-Three

The Children Have a Home

Before breakfast four businessmen arrived to progress negotiations for the land by the sea. They admitted that the doctor who owned the land and the buildings associated with it had had a business failure and wanted to dispose of it, but would really like to see David using it for his work. That sounded as though they were trying to work on David's good nature. They were asking for twelve laks rupees, which was more than David wanted to pay, and more than had been intimated in the last phone call; not only that, they wanted an additional two laks rupees for utility costs. David was quite firm on this since he knew the figure God had given him and he told them to come back only when the figure was ten laks rupees in total.

David told us he was still in favour of one of the other sites.

Later that morning, whilst we were resting, the businessmen called David to tell him the doctor had agreed to the price of ten laks rupees inclusive. That is less than £20,000. We rejoiced together at this wonderful news.

Praise God from whom all blessings flow!

The doctor had also agreed that David could move the children on to the site immediately. All he needed now was the money to pay for it all and to negotiate the payment terms.

David told us of his feelings on the fifty years of independence in India. Independence, he thought, has done nothing for India and

97

its people. There are no foreign missionaries, the Government is inadequate and nothing is done to prevent the continuation of the caste system. The poor are squeezed more and more and ignored by higher society. Road construction has stagnated for fifty years. There are many who are sad that the British left India, particularly the poor people. Ghandi called them 'God's people' but they were outcast, not even allowed a vote.

We waited around all afternoon expecting the arrival of the doctor who was selling the land. He was expected between 3.00pm and 4.00pm. 4.00pm came and went but with no sign of the doctor so we continued to wait. He arrived at 5.00pm and David asked if we could take the children over there this afternoon. They had other matters to discuss concerning the site and by 6.00pm all was agreed.

David decided to collect everything together, take the children and their carers over there, and consecrate the site to the glory of God. This is a man of action. If you can do it now, why wait? It seemed risky to us since we had a train to catch at 10.00pm and Jemima would be preparing dinner for us before then.

They piled into the jeep, as many as possible, and the remainder set off for the service bus. David said that they would arrive at the site in 'about forty minutes'. We would see; I was certain he was measuring that in Indian time.

It was 6.30pm when we left in the jeep and about 7.00pm when we arrived at site. The doctor and one of his associates arrived shortly after us. It was dark, the stars were shining brightly and there was a new moon with light shining all around it like a ring. We walked across the site by torchlight and as we did so, Charlis set off in the jeep to meet the service bus and bring the others.

As we waited, the three of us walked on the beach. We could hardly see any sand for the thousands of sand crabs which scuttled away whenever the torch light shone on them. I thought just how the children would worry the life out of these sand crabs.

The doctor and his friend opened the doors of a building to reveal a small room in which the children would sleep. There was no electricity; that had been cut off due to non-payment, and it would have to be sorted out. The staff brought propane gas lamps and storm lamps and lit up the room.

It was well turned 8.00pm when Charlis returned with the others.

We gathered together outside the door of the dormitory and I opened proceedings with a prayer. Leonard read some lessons about little children. He thanked the doctor and his friend for their part in making all this possible. Then Robert cut the tape and in we went to present to each child a blanket and some sweets. They would be sleeping on the concrete floor until such time as David could arrange for some beds. That would be normal for them.

The doctor made a wonderful gesture. He promised to be doctor to all these children, to visit them at least once each week, and to do it free of charge. His heart had been warmed.

There is a school nearby and David would arrange for the children to attend there. That would help them to integrate.

This was a fitting end to our stay in Chirala.

We returned to Baerpet by 9.00pm and Jemima produced dinner for us. We had tomato soup followed by chicken pieces with rice. It was lovely.

By 9.30pm we were ready to leave for the railway station and off we set. We were in good time for the 10.00pm train but we waited and waited until Dhamaros brought us the news that the train was four hours late. We said our farewells and sent everybody home and then sat in the waiting room. We had been concerned that going to see the children settled might cause us to miss the train, and here we were waiting another four hours. We would have been disappointed if we had missed out on that wonderful blessing.

Blessing Twenty-Four

Return to Madras

As this day started, we were still at Chirala railway station, trying to sleep in the waiting room. We managed a cat-nap and a Christian gentleman came to speak to us for a while. He seemed to know about the big evangelical meetings in Hyderabad, with well-known evangelists such as Derek Prince and Maurice Cerello.

There was a young boy sleeping on a table in the waiting room. The table was hard but he was fast asleep. He was a homeless boy, without parents or family. These are the children David wants to help. It is very much like the conditions which prevailed when those saints of the past set up the children's homes in London. David said he would seek out this young boy when he returned and offer him a place in his seaside home.

The train arrived at 2.00am and our compartment was clear. Hallelujah! This seemed better than last time. Was it our experiences over the last three weeks that made it seem so, or was it the glass in the windows? We each chose a bench and off we went to sleep.

We all awoke at about 6.15am, still some way short of Madras, but it was light and we were able to see some of the scenery until we reached our destination some time after 8.00am.

In spite of pressure from several porters at the station, we carried our own cases to the taxi. David tried to negotiate a price with one porter but the porter would not indicate a price so David told him, 'no price, no deal'. We had learned a lesson last time. We were brought directly to the YWCA and David booked a room. Leonard and Robert would be catching their plane that same day, so we only needed the one room.

After breakfast of toast and jam we set off in two three-wheeled taxis through the mayhem of Madras to Thomas Cooks. I cashed my remaining £100 in travellers' cheques and David cashed the $3,000 cheques which Leonard had given him. There was a mountain of paper even in large denomination notes. Robert had a brief case and put all the money in it. This is a fortune in India, more than one lak rupees (100,000 rupees).

Robert managed to confirm his flight so I asked about mine. Apparently Air India flights were off the screen at the moment but they said they would ring YWCA when the flight was confirmed. The British Airways flight from Bombay was OK. We set off in search of a bank to deposit the mountain of money in Robert's brief case. It was like those old films in which thieves kept the money they had stolen in brief cases. We went to three banks before we found one which would accept the money, and that exercise was long and tedious. The money had to be divided into three parts but in the end David had a bankers' draft for more money than he needed for the down payment on the property by the sea, where the children had awoken for the first time that morning.

After lunch I rang you. Your tests had gone well and you were planning a walk in Roundhay Park, Leeds with Molly. Friday was so near now and we could look forward to it with joy. Then we rested until about 4.15pm, when I rang Thomas Cooks, since I had heard nothing from them. There was no reply.

During the afternoon we had rested. Our room had the luxury of air-conditioning but David was shivering, so we had to turn the air conditioning off. It reminded me of an African friend who stayed with us and whom we had found having a bath in the middle of the night in order to warm himself.

By 7.00pm Tony and Judith had not arrived. We waited until

7.30pm and then had dinner. I chose western-style, which was fish and chips with bread and butter. That was OK and I enjoyed it although the fish could hardly compare with the beautiful fleshy haddock we have in Yorkshire.

Tony and Judith arrived at 8.30pm. It was really good to see them. They had yet to eat, but they said they would be happy to eat out. We talked to them about David and his work. Tony seemed to be very interested in helping David, even to the extent of doing so on his days off in Vellore. There would be no pastoral support from Vellore since only Tony and Judith, together with one other, represent the Baptist Church there.

Spiritual things here are in the hands of the Church of South India. Perhaps that is the route David will have to take. We shall see about that.

The time came for Leonard and Robert to go to the airport so Tony and Judith left to find somewhere to eat, and the four of us set off in a taxi for the airport. Our parting from Leonard and Robert was swift, a quick shake of the hands and off they went into the airport. We tried to confirm my flight but we were unsuccessful.

On the way back to the YWCA, the taxi windscreen shattered, hit by a stone. The driver brought us back with his head way out of the window, through as many back streets as he could find. When he dropped us off, he tried to get David to pay for the replacement window. It was a blessing for us to have an Indian guide.

Blessing Twenty-Five

THURSDAY, 4TH DECEMBER, 1997

The Return Home

We met Tony and Judith at breakfast and enjoyed our chat. It was good for them, not only because they knew me but because they have so few opportunities to speak to Westerners. We talked about David and his work and about them and their work in Vellore. Tony and Judith showed a real interest in David's work, particularly in the development by the sea. It would provide Tony with an additional interest in India and he expressed a desire to go and see it. This was what I had been hoping and praying for.

Tony and Judith went off to do some shopping and I asked if she could buy me some small presents to bring back for our elderly relatives. We remained in the YWCA in order that I might try to confirm my flights. Contact with British Airways was easy and they were able to confirm what I already knew about Bombay to London, but I would have to contact Air India for the internal flight to Bombay. That was easier said than done. It took a long time to get through to Air India but eventually I did so. It was just as well. The flight had been brought forward by two hours and I had to be at the airport by 4.15pm.

We rested for a while and then went down for lunch, just in time to meet Tony and Judith returning from their shopping expedition. Judith had managed to buy me some silk scarves which were just right. They asked me to bring back their Christmas cards, which I did.

We had lunch together and continued our conversation. They

have another four years in India and will not be coming to England until 1999. I hope they will be able to find time to come and see us. In any event they promised to keep us informed of their involvement in Chirala. They sent their best wishes to all their friends at home. They have given up much in giving five years of their lives for this work. They deserve our prayers and will have them.

At 3.00pm Tony and Judith left to catch the bus back to Vellore. They wanted to return before dark as that road is notorious for robberies; like Jerusalem to Jericho.

I had a shower, shave and change of clothing for the journey home. David ordered a taxi and off we set for the airport.

This was the first time we had travelled between Madras and the airport in daylight and it seemed so different, though much busier of course.

I went straight to the booking-in desk and was told that I would have to collect my luggage at Bombay (Mumbai), which was different from what I had expected, but the booking was straightforward. I went back to the area where I had left David. He was waiting for me, so I told him all was well and we said our goodbyes. He was returning to Chirala on the night train. What a good host he had been! He is a fine Christian man.

The flight was much earlier than published, 5.45pm instead of 7.50pm, and we were in Mumbai by 7.30pm. Here there was a free bus waiting to take us to the International Airport quite a distance away. In Bombay the traffic was heavy but more ordered than in Madras and soon we were at the International Airport.

The British Airways desk was first in the terminal but was closed because it was so early before my flight. The desk opened at about 9.30pm and I was second in the queue. I was given a good window seat and booked right through to Manchester, with another good window seat from Heathrow to Manchester. As I understood it, I would have to collect my luggage at Heathrow and take it through customs. I misunderstood that as I found out later.

By 10.00pm I had cleared customs and gone through to International Space with about four more hours to flight time. I sat in a quiet spot and brought my diary up to date.

The flight from Bombay to Heathrow was comfortable enough, except that midway through the flight I felt very cold in spite of having a blanket. The gentleman blocking my way to the aisle was fast asleep and there were no stewards about, so I shivered for some time until a passing steward handed me my jacket from the rack and said he would put the heat up a little. The only meal on the flight was a rather pleasant breakfast, not long before we arrived at Heathrow.

I was off the plane very quickly and managed to ring you to confirm my arrival. You said that the flight to Manchester had been delayed slightly and you would be there in time to meet me.

I went to collect my luggage and I watched all the other luggage go round and round the carousel. Eventually I asked a passing British Airways employee what was going on and it seemed that my luggage had been taken direct to the domestic terminal. It was getting near time for the departure of my plane so I dashed to catch the airport bus and arrived in time for the flight.

How I enjoyed that flight over England's green and pleasant land, light snow over the hills! I had left Bombay in an evening temperature of 29 degrees celsius and arrived in London in a morning temperature below zero, but it was wonderful.

The customs officials were expecting me and asked a few questions before letting me through to where you were waiting with our daughter Suzanne and granddaughter Hannah. The time had arrived and it was wonderful. Thank you for letting me go and thank you for your lovely welcome home.

David's Vision

Gospel Work

Church Plantation
(Construction)
in rural areas

School of Evangelism
(Bible School) – future

Film Ministry
(Jesus film only)

Radio Ministry (future)
(already trained in this)

Pastoral support of
evangelists (future)

Support for independent
pastors and lay workers
with no formal education

Sunday School support
(future)

Gospel meetings
(as we have been doing)

Tracts, Literature, Bible
printing press (future)

Youth evangelism

Community Development Programmes

– Community
  Saving schemes

– Fisheries (Sea and Inland)

– Agriculture

– Literacy
  (formal and non-formal)

– Water and Sanitation

– Disabled orphans

– Health Clinics

– Help for elderly abused

– Youth programmes

– Leadership camps for
  villagers

– Assessment of problems
  and alternatives

– Day care centres
  (future)

– Shelter for homeless
  (housing programmes)
  (future)

– School drop-outs

– alcohol, drugs,
  HIV/AIDS advice (future)

Reflections

Before leaving for India, I had a vision, a very clear picture. In my vision I was a lump of wet clay in the hands of God and as I watched, He formed me into the shape of India. In God's hands I had been transformed from my own shape to become India-shaped. At about the same time, our Minister, John, was seeking ideas for a logo for the Church to which we belong and I had an image of God's hands holding an empty Cross with people sitting around its foot.

When I arrived in Chirala and saw David's jeep for the first time, I was amazed to see the Redemption logo on the jeep door. It was an image of God's hands enfolding a map of India. There was no way that I could have known that until the moment I saw it in Chirala. It was confirmation, if ever I needed it, of my calling to minister in India.

There were several other 'coincidences'. Throughout our time in India it rained quite often, but we were never rained on when ministering and yet, the moment we left, there were torrential downpours, as a result of which ten people in the area died. While we were visiting the Chinsu tribe, there was an explosion of the transformer supplying power to the village, but not before we had preached and the people responding to the message had done so and been prayed for. In Kroth Palem our jeep was set alight but there were no burn marks or faults in the jeep. In the time of our visit the price for the land and buildings by the sea fell from forty laks rupees to ten laks rupees, the site was purchased and the disabled children housed there. Some might think all these are coincidences. I believe they are God's confirmation of our ministry, that He is at the heart of it and it is all in His hands.

But this image of the hands of God forming me into the shape of India has left a deep impression on me and this has been reinforced by the Redemption logo. I was held in the hands of God and formed by Him into the shape of India. There would be no Western influence in my ministry. I would be coming alongside Indian people in their situation, in their joys and sadnesses, in their poverty and difficulties, in their experience of life. I would be entering into their culture, sharing with them in it, and applying the Christian Gospel to their situation.

Some of the first people we met in Chirala were the disabled children and I remember particularly that mentally disturbed little girl who was laid at my feet. What could I do to help her? How could I identify with her, become her shape? I was lost even for words. I did the best I could, which was to pray for her and her mother. I felt helpless and all I could do was to put her into the hands of God. The physically disabled children were around also, sleeping rough around David's house. How could we come alongside them? We encouraged David in finding accommodation for them and before we left, we had the honour of opening the buildings which are now housing them and in presenting the children with their blankets. Then all we could do was to leave them in the hands of God and the people He has called to care for them. We saw all those children who were begging on the streets and in the trains, many with hardly any clothing on them. What could we do for them? Nothing.

We visited the leper colony and looked around in tears. How could I possibly become leper-shaped? I didn't even touch any. All we could do was to visit them, to smile, hold our hands together in peace and pray God's blessing on them. We could only leave them in the hands of God and those who were committed to helping them.

When we visited the Chinsu and stayed two nights in Dornala, we were shocked by the standard of our accommodation. This was a really backward area. The main street was muddy, the area outside our room crowded with beds for people sleeping in the open air. Our room was so small, with just room for two single bunks for the three of us, a doorway to the outside and one into our Indian toilet with tap. Below the balcony outside our door was an open drain and food was being prepared alongside it. We might have thought we were identifying with the people, but to them our accommodation would have been luxury. In no way could we say we had taken on their shape.

Yet they were thankful that we had come, all those people we visited, wherever we went. I think that they thought we had identified with them. It seems that they were thankful simply that we had been to see them and spend a while with them, to be identified with their plight and all that was being done to help them, both physically and spiritually.

What then is the point of the vision? I think it is to show just how much God has identified with them, and also with us, in Jesus. That was the point in our preaching and is an important reflection on my visit for us as well.

As I am writing these notes, I can see through our patio window the shape of India in a puddle being formed by the rain. As the puddle is growing, there is light rain falling on it. This is part of the picture. It is God who has India in His hands. That might seem strange with 98% of the population not acknowledging Him as God, but still His rain falls on it, a picture of the love and grace which He showers on it in Christ. God has India in His hands and is using David Raju and his team and those of us who have visited them to bring the good news of His love to these needy people, to bring them into His Kingdom and help them live as princes and princesses of the Kingdom. He has even used us in our inadequacy and weakness. He had us in His hands throughout our stay and He did the work which He sent us to do.

Of course, the whole purpose of our visit was to present to them our Lord and Saviour and to invite them to accept Him as their Lord and Saviour. He is the One who has identified, and always will identify, with them in whatever situation they find themselves. He was the One sent to spend a season with us, not three weeks and a few days but thirty-three years. One fitting logo for Jesus would be God's hands holding the form of man into which shape Jesus was made. This would be a true picture because Jesus has identified with us perfectly. He has identified with all the poor people we met in India, with all those little children begging or working for a pittance or those disabled or living in the leper colony, with all those who have nowhere to lay their head.

Jesus came to us in poverty, in a borrowed stable among the straw and animals. In His birth He was treated no better than an animal. I have often thought that many people in India are worse off than animals. Jesus often had to sleep rough during His ministry in conditions far worse than we experienced in Dornala.

Jesus was able to identify with all He met, whatever their need, the poor and blind, the lame, the sick, the dying and those afflicted with leprosy. He was able to touch them and heal them. He was able to identify with those cast out by society, tax collectors, a woman taken in adultery, a woman who had had five husbands when even the man she was living with wasn't her husband, with two criminals on the crosses beside His. He identifies with everybody whatever their need.

Yet we still haven't touched the most significant identification of Jesus. It is true that He has identified with us and still does, but He not only takes on our shape, He has taken on Himself our sin, even though He was and is, and always will be sinless and has become sin-shaped in order to deal with it. That was the whole point of His coming among us, in order that He might deal with sin once and for all. Jesus became sin-shaped for us.

It was in Gethsemane that Jesus faced the consequence of becoming sin-shaped. The consequence was the Cross, for that was the price that had to be paid to the Holy God. 'Father, take this cup away from Me,' He cried, His human shape recoiling at the pain and suffering that the Cross held; 'Yet, not My will but Yours be done.' In obedience He was trusting in God in spite of the agony which faced Him.

Being other-people-shaped is never easy. There is pain and there is conflict; there is suffering. For Jesus, becoming human-shaped meant a Cross and He went to that Cross in obedience to the will and purpose of God.

From the Cross Jesus was able to cry out in triumph, 'It is finished!' He had finished the work God had given Him to do. He had become man-shaped and sin-shaped and had paid the price. It was finished.

Of course we know that God, the Father, agreed that it was finished by raising our Saviour to the highest heaven, to His right hand where our Saviour reigns in glory and from where He will come again.

In Matthew 8 verse 19 there is the story of the teacher of the law who came to Jesus saying that He would follow Jesus wherever He went. Jesus responded by telling him that foxes have holes and birds have nests but He, the Son of Man, had nowhere to lay His head.

Following Jesus is never an easy ride. It can lead us to the most uncomfortable situations. We are reminded of it every year in our Covenant Service and I never really understood what I was promising until I had been to India. In it we invite God to put us to what He desires, with whom He desires, doing or suffering, employed or laid aside, exalted or brought low, full or empty, having everything or nothing. We are giving God an open cheque to do what He wills with our lives. It is putting complete trust in Him to control our lives as He wills; just as Jesus did.

Let nobody ever believe that being a Christian frees anybody from pain or suffering. Being a Christian is never easy.

The truth is that Christian people are Christ's representatives on earth. We are His hands, His feet and His voice. It is true that of ourselves we can never do what He did but I remember His promise to His disciples that they would do even greater things than He did as a result of His returning to His Father. Even the Hindu policeman could tell David Raju that he would do greater things than these. Why can we do greater things than Jesus did? Because we believe in Him and have the power and authority of the Holy Spirit. The power doesn't come from us; it is within us by the Spirit of God. He accomplishes His work through us by His Spirit. Our calling as Christians is to be among others, taking on their shape, meeting them at their point of need and letting the grace of God flow to them through us. In our weakness He makes us strong.

St Paul knew all about the need to take on the shape of others and spelled it out in 1 Corinthians 9 verses 19-23. He says that he made himself a slave in order to save as many as possible. To the Jews he was a Jew, to Gentiles a Gentile, to the weak he became weak in order to win the weak. He became all things to all people in order that he might save some. He did it not for himself but for the sake of the Gospel. He was saying that he had to take on the shape of others in order to win them for Christ.

It seems to me that the problem with the Church today is that it has adopted a shape and welcomes people into it providing they are happy to take on that shape. This is completely at odds with the Gospel. It is at odds with what Jesus did and taught, with what St Paul did and with what we are called to do. We are called to become other-people-shaped, to meet them where they are, in their experience of life, even if it shocks us, and to identify with them in their culture. Our place is in the world even if we are not of it.

We are not here to satisfy ourselves. We are representatives of the Kingdom to bring the Gospel to others.

This might well be a frightening prospect. I am sure that Jesus was afraid in Gethsemane. His feelings there were true human feelings; otherwise He would not have identified with us. It is never easy. It will never be easy but we have the power of God at our disposal. We are in His hands and He will see us through.

St John had that wonderful vision recorded in the Book of Revelation. In that vision he heard the risen Christ speak to the Church at Laodicea. (Revelation 3 v 14ff) In it Jesus accuses the Church of being lukewarm, neither hot nor cold and says that He will spit them out of His mouth. I wonder whether 'lukewarm' would describe the Church to which we belong? Do we sit comfortably in our pews? Is our Christian life about attending Church week by week, singing a few hymns and songs, saying or listening to a few prayers, listening to a sermon? Have we formed ourselves into a nice, comfortable shape which suits our view of Christianity? Are we disturbed when somebody tries a new pattern of worship so as to bring it more into line with what is happening outside? Are we disturbed even if somebody sits in our pew? I wonder how we would react if a dropout of society, a punk or a beggar, attended our services? I fear that we are little different from the Church of Laodicea.

Jesus says, 'Stop! Wake up! Let Me take you and shape you. Let Me control your life and your thinking. Let Me use you for the extension of My Kingdom. Let Me fill you and set you on fire with My Holy Spirit, to live and to serve Me in the world. It won't be easy but the rewards are out of this world.'

In the end we will be able to say, 'It is finished' with conviction and hear God's 'Amen' as we are raised to be with Him for ever.

It is quite something to let God mould us into the shape He wants us to take. I pray that we and all our Christian friends will allow Him to do that.

Valedictory Address

My brothers and sisters in Christ.

We have been in India now for three weeks. In that time we have been privileged to see many things.

Madras was a culture shock for us with all the noise, mad traffic and animals all over the place. I would much rather live in the countryside around Chirala than in Madras. We have seen beautiful countryside and lovely people who have greeted us with open arms wherever we have gone. We have been showered with the love and good wishes of all whom we have met, always being asked to return some day.

We have seen many things that have saddened us. We have been to a leper colony in which people have no hope of coming out, even small children who do not have leprosy. We have seen young children working or begging. There are no school facilities for them.

We have seen people using grass verges as toilets, open for all to see, and we have heard of their feelings of embarrassment at having to do so.

We have seen outcast people who have no hope, due to a caste system which restricts them and threatens a worse after-life if they rebel.

We have been in a country in which 98% of the population do not know Jesus Christ as Lord and have no hope, not only in this life but also in the life to come.

We have found that the caste system is alive and well even in the Christian Church. This must be the first place from which it is removed. If Christians do nothing about it, nobody else will.

It has been our joy and a real privilege to be with a group of people who are doing something about all these social and spiritual wrongs. All that we have seen of your work has been special to us.

We have seen children being educated, disabled children being cared for. We have seen fishing and shepherding communities given hope by helping them build community businesses, and we have seen the pride on their faces at their success.

We have seen water and sanitation programmes and seen the joy in the people who are benefiting from them. We have seen health and hygiene education programmes.

Church building programmes have been a joy to see and in our time here more than two thousand have been added to the Church.

All this is being done through this group of twenty-five people. We find your work awesome, all for the glory of God our Father.

To you, our dear friends in Christ, all that I feel I can say to you is to apply to you words spoken by the Apostle Paul to his friend Timothy, to, 'fan into flame the gift of God which is within you'. (2 Timothy 1 verse 6)

Read the Scriptures diligently, pray without ceasing, meet together for fellowship and strengthening. Get all the additional training you can to improve your effectiveness.

We will pray for you. Your work is outstanding. God bless you all.

Hannah's Letter

16th November, 1997

Dear Granddad,

Grandma has told me that you have got to India safely and that everybody gave you flowers when you arrived. She also said that you had been speaking in tongues. I can already do that so maybe we can have a talk when you get back! My teeth have been hurting me lately, now I have eight and Mummy and Daddy will be glad when I finally get them all through. I can now feed myself at dinner time when I have my sandwich. It's nice to feel the bread though before I put it in my mouth. When I put it in my mouth everybody has got to clap because I'm such a clever girl. I have also started to drink my juice by myself but it is hard to tip my beaker properly. I might be better at it by the time you get back. Don't worry about Grandma because I will help to look after her and keep her company. I'll have to go now because the paper is running out. Mummy and Daddy send their love and I'll see you at the airport.

Lots of love and kisses,

Hannah

David Raju's Letter

20th December, 1997

Dear Bro. Grahame,

Greetings in the precious Name of our Lord and Saviour, Jesus Christ the soon coming King.

I would like to thank you personally for visiting India along with Bro. Nash and Bro. Robert, having trust on me. It was thrilling experience for us to work with you when you were here and we proved as good ground. We laughed, we smiled and preached. We thanked God as our hearts felt joy for the Lord's work. I have been dreaming for the last twenty years about the unique work of the Lord. Sometimes I felt like a 'cry in the wilderness' but now I have a ray of hope, a way to reach the unreached through our Ministry supporters for the noble work that God has called us to do. I know it's a hard way and unending journey but with the mighty strength and wisdom of our Lord we will do the Lord's work with our team.

It's wonderful to note that we have taken the Gospel to the remote areas where they have never heard of Jesus before. The Spirit of the Lord moved upon the people and the Hindu people accepted Jesus as their personal Saviour. What a wonderful job we did for the Lord. It's remarkable. You have seen what I am doing with our team but we are still on the way. We have to cross many milestones. Please pray for our spiritual journey. We have to overcome many hurdles.

His cause has allowed us to proclaim the love of Christ to people in the massive fields. We have challenged from the Satan in this country. I will continue to serve the Lord. For this purpose I live. We need your prayer support.

As you are aware the harvest is plenty but the labourers are few. I trust that you will rejoice with our ministry for the fruit of the harvest. At the same time I pray your heart will be challenged for the work that is yet to be done.

A heartful of gratitude goes out to you who have given generously to Redemption ministries and prayed for our work in Andhra Pradesh, India. To your credit we have touched eternity together, and we are just getting started.

Thank you for your love, thank you for your prayers, phone calls. We are happy that you safely arrived in England. We are still praying for your health because you were in a foreign land like India where there is no good food or proper facilities but for the Lord's work you bore all these things. Thanks a lot for your patience.

We wanted to see you again and again in this land because the harvest calls. We honour you. I am missing you a lot. The disabled children are well. They send love to you and my wonderful family and staff join with them to say to you and Marion a happy and Christ filled Christmas season now and all through the coming year.

Our special thanks to Marion and your family who allowed you to stay in India for three weeks. Please let me know anything you are not able to trace out of your belongings so that I can send them or bring them along with me when I come to England.

We are happy to read the letter of Marion dated 4th December, 1997. Please convey our thanks to Marion and your granddaughter who wrote a very interesting letter while you were here.

We have had heavy rains after you left and Ongole was inundated and about ten people died in our district. It's amazing our work wasn't hampered during your visit.

After you left I had a press meeting and our daily newspapers published about your trip and it was good.

Your sincerely in Christ Jesus,

A. David Raju

Postscript

Following my visit to India, we began to seek ways of raising funds to help with the development of the site by the sea. An appeal was made to the members of the Church we attend and as a result we were able to send a cheque for £2,000. We also showed my slides of the visit and further presentations are being arranged.

The editor of our local newspaper became interested in the visit and arranged for the first slide show to be reported, with a photograph of the two of us in Indian clothing, and this was followed by an interview with me on my visit.

I then wrote to David Raju informing him of the local interest and sent copies of the newspaper articles. The following letter was received in response and you will understand my delight in receiving it.

'Dear Bro Dixon and Marion,

It's a great blessing to us to receive your wonderful letter dated 8th April, 1998.

We enjoyed the articles about your visit to India published in your local newspaper. I thank you for the same.

I am also ever grateful to The Central Methodist and United Reformed Church. Please continue to pray for our work in our area and also for the registration of the site near the sea coast.

During Easter Tony and Judith visited us and we had a wonderful time. They were here for three days from Good Friday to Easter.

Myself and Tony spoke on the last sayings of Jesus in the Lutheran church and on the same day at our Church on the sea coast (at the new site). Tony, Judith, myself, Jemima, Charlis and disabled children project staff spoke on each word of our Lord from the Cross. It was a wonderful day.

Again, on Easter Sunday Tony gave the message of the Resurrection of Christ. Jemima and myself presented Indian dress to Tony and Judith. Tony told me he would be using his engineering skills for the construction of the Church and the home for the handicapped children. We had a love feast on Easter Sunday with our 110 Church members. Among thirty disabled children sixteen have undergone surgery and are recovering day by day. They are all learning well both in school and Sunday School.

Our new Church has grown so quickly and now we have a congregation of more than one hundred members. Please pray for them to grow in the faith of the Lord.

It is lovely to see you both in your Indian dress and please send a big size photograph of that to keep in our house. It is a great joy for us to have relationship with you through Jesus Christ and I pray that through this bond our Lord must be glorified.

Our best wishes to your family and church members.

With regards,
Yours in His service.
A. David Raju'

The months which followed were difficult for Redemption. The deposit had been paid on the land by the sea but it was necessary to raise funds quickly to pay the sum outstanding. That proved more difficult than had been hoped and there was a real danger of the land being taken from them. However by some miracle the funds were raised due to the efforts of Leonard Nash and the property was eventually signed over to Redemption Ministries.

In January, 1999 Leonard Nash led another visit to Chirala and following that visit he was able to send out the following letter.

Postscript

The Rev Bill Luther of Love and Truth Church (Adamsville, Tennessee), Chuck Tatum of Unity Broadcasting Channel 18, David Whitlow and myself have just returned from our second crusade in India. It was awesome!

In the first crusade, 'Setting Sun Ministries' (Leonard's charity) made the down payment on two acres of land and nine buildings on the Sea of Bengal and immediately helped to establish a school for thirty handicapped teenagers, thirteen- to fifteen-year-olds, with two full-time teachers, cooks and caretaker. The crude buildings would never pass inspection in USA but there it happened! The youth were so unpromising; could anything be made of their twisted bodies and broken spirits? In God's hands there is healing for soul, mind and body.

David Raju saw the crippled teenagers not able to attend school and God gave him a plan. David talked to parents and guardians and asked that they be given into the care of Redemption Ministries for three years. They would be loved and cared for during this time with shelter, food, clothing, medical (aid), and educated with some trade. The whole purpose is to lead them to know Jesus and to equip them with skills for life. Is it working? Yes! Yes! Yes!

I was anxious in January, 1999 to see how they had progressed in one year. Wow! Unbelievable. They are alive in Christ, in joy, in excitement. Sixteen have had major surgery, others given braces and medication. They shared songs and Scripture in English. When asked if their parents were Hindu, all shook their heads, 'Yes', but at the same time they began to say, 'Not us, we are Christian, we follow Jesus Christ.' Our thinking is, give us a teenager for three years and surround him/her with the love of Christ and fully teach them God's word, then we can send them home as a missionary for Jesus.

121

This year has been a miracle year in other ways also. The school property has been paid for in full. More than two hundred people have been meeting each Sunday for worship on the campus even though there was no building. Because of your gifts we were able to build a Church building that will seat 2,000 to 2,500 people. I expect this congregation to grow to about 500 this year. On 24th January we dedicated this Church to the glory of God. I named this Church 'Shiloh Chapel' (Place of Rest, Gen 49:10; Josh 18:10; Judges 18:31)

Bryan Gammill and his wife, Sarah are there as missionaries from the state of Washington, USA. It is Bryan's vision to staff a Bible School on the campus for training local pastors and adult Sunday School teachers. Please pray for the Bible School, the fields are white unto harvest.'

... etc ... etc.

Since I left India following the first visit, Tony and Judith Sykes have spent all their spare time with David Raju. They have provided for a water pump and piping to bring fresh water to the site and Tony has prepared all the construction drawings for the new Church and accommodation, including all estimates of construction costs. This is a wonderful extension of my ministry in India.

In May, 1999 Marion and I visited Leonard at his home in Tennessee. There I was able to share with many people the work in India and to meet up with Robert Old, Bill Luther, Chuck Tatum and David Whitlow. I took with me fifty copies of my book and gave it to those who made a gift offering for India. During the time we were there we were given $6,250, all of which was sent to India making approximately $70,000 sent by Leonard and Central Church, Batley over the past year. The total estimated cost to enable the campus to function is $100,000.

When I was in America I found out that one Church, the First

Baptist Church of Marmaduke, Arkansas, is sponsoring the new Church for the Lembadi tribe and has sent a gift of almost $4,400. The Pastor of that church intends to visit India with Leonard on the next trip. My estimates of the number involved in the Lembadi tribe were woefully short. It appears that more than twice the number were converted that night than on the day of Pentecost. Seven villages including about 10,000 people were involved and a new Church for 1,500 is to be constructed. That will not be adequate and it is hoped that another four Churches will be provided in time.

Love and Truth Church in Adamsville, Tennessee has sent a substantial gift of more than $5,000 for use where it is needed.

Whilst in America, Leonard and I were interviewed on TV by Chuck and Vicky Tatum and that created considerable interest.

What is happening is wonderful. It is clearly within God's will and purpose and even more wonderful things will be seen in the future.

Gifts for the work of Redemption Ministries
in India can be sent as follows:

1. In American Dollars to:
   Setting Sun Ministries,
   5420, Highway 128 S,
   SAVANNAH,
   TENNESSEE 38372,
   USA.
   (Cheques payable to 'Setting Sun Ministries')

2. In Sterling to:
   Ce   Batley,
   (i   is for India)
   Ce   ted Reformed Church,
   Co
   BATLEY,
   West Yorkshire,
   England,
   UK.

GRAHAME & MARION DIXON
104 WOODFIELD AVENUE
STAINCLIFFE
BATLEY
WF17 7DX
TEL: 472891